# Modern Concurrency

## in Swift

By Marin Todorov

# Modern Concurrency in Swift

By Marin Todorov

Copyright ©2021 Razeware LLC.

## Notice of Rights

## Notice of Liability

## Trademarks

ISBN: 978-1-950325-53-5

# Table of Contents

# Book License

By purchasing *Modern Concurrency in Swift*, you have the following license:

- You are allowed to use and/or modify the source code in *Modern Concurrency in Swift* in as many apps as you want, with no attribution required.

- You are allowed to use and/or modify all art, images and designs that are included in *Modern Concurrency in Swift* in as many apps as you want, but must include this attribution line somewhere inside your app: "Artwork/images/designs: from *Modern Concurrency in Swift*, available at www.raywenderlich.com".

- The source code included in *Modern Concurrency in Swift* is for your personal use only. You are NOT allowed to distribute or sell the source code in *Modern Concurrency in Swift* without prior authorization.

- This book is for your personal use only. You are NOT allowed to sell this book without prior authorization, or distribute it to friends, coworkers or students; they would need to purchase their own copies.

# Before You Begin

This section tells you a few things you need to know before you get started, such as what you'll need for hardware and software, where to find the project files for this book, and more.

# What You Need

To follow along with this book, you'll need the following:

- A Mac running **macOS Monterey (12.0)** or later. Big Sur should work, but this book was written and tested on macOS Monterey, so your mileage may vary.

- **Xcode 13 or later**. Xcode is the main development tool for iOS. You'll need Xcode 13 or newer for the tasks in this book. If you're using Xcode 13.2 and above, the new async/await syntax and the rest of the modern concurrency features will work starting with iOS 13 / macOS 10.15 SDK (or later). If you're using an older version of Xcode 13, you'll only get modern concurrency support when targeting iOS 15 / macOS 12. You can download the latest version of Xcode from Apple's developer site (https://apple.co/2asi58y)

- **An intermediate level of Swift**. Concurrency in general is a relatively advanced topic, so you need to have at least an intermediate-level knowledge of Swift and its existing concurrency features. This book won't teach pre-Swift 5.5 Concurrency features such as Grand Central Dispatch, but you should still be able to follow the contents of this book, even if you're not entirely proficient with them.

This book does **not** require a physical device. However, you might want to try some of the advanced concurrency features on a real device, so you can truly feel how it works in "the real world".

# Book Source Code & Forums

## Where to download the materials for this book

The materials for this book can be cloned or downloaded from the GitHub book materials repository:

- https://github.com/raywenderlich/mcon-materials/tree/editions/1.0

## Forums

We've also set up an official forum for the book at https://forums.raywenderlich.com/c/books/modern-concurrency-in-swift. This is a great place to ask questions about the book or to submit any errors you may find.

"Dedicated to my daughter and family. Warm thanks to everyone on the extended team that made this book possible."

— *Marin Todorov*

# About the Authors

 **Marin Todorov** is a developer, speaker and author. He works for high-profile clients, most often doing Swift development.Besides crafting code, he enjoys blogging, writing books, teaching and speaking. He sometimes open-sources his code.More about Marin at: https://www.underplot.com

# About the Editors

 **Rich Turton** is a tech editor for this book. He's been developing apps for Apple platforms since before it was cool. He lives in the UK with his wife, daughters and terrible cat.

 **Felipe Laso Marsetti** is a tech editor for this book. He's a Technical Lead working at Lextech Global Services. In his spare time, Felipe enjoys learning new languages and frameworks, playing violin and guitar, cooking and also video games. You can follow him on Twitter as @iFeliLM (https://twitter.com/iFeliLM) or on his blog at https://programmer.pink.

 **Sandra Grauschopf** is the editor of this book. She's a freelance writer, editor, and content strategist as well as the Editing Team Lead at raywenderlich.com. She loves to untangle tortured sentences and to travel the world with a trusty book in her hand. You can follow her on Twitter at https://twitter.com/sgrauschopf or learn more about her at https://grauschopf.com.

 **Shai Mishali** is the final pass editor on this book. He's an experienced, award-winning iOS specialist, an international speaker and a highly active open-source contributor and maintainer on several high-profile projects. He works on the RxSwift Community and RxSwift projects, but also releases many open-source endeavors around Combine such as CombineCocoa, RxCombine and more. As an avid enthusiast of hackathons, Shai took first place at BattleHack Tel-Aviv 2014, BattleHack World Finals San Jose 2014 and Ford's Developer Challenge Tel-Aviv 2015. You can find him on GitHub (https://github.com/freak4pc) and Twitter as @freak4pc (https://twitter.com/freak4pc).

# Acknowledgments

We would like to thank Audrey Tam, Marin Benčević and Piotr Fulmanski for their help in reviewing portions of this book and providing their feedback.

# Introduction

Welcome to *Modern Concurrency in Swift*, the book that walks you through the amazing new concurrency APIs introduced in Swift 5.5.

Swift is a powerful, all-purpose programming language that's currently expanding beyond Apple's platforms (like iOS, macOS, tvOS and so on) and into new platforms like Linux, Windows, and more.

To help the language take on a whole new set of tasks, Swift 5.5 introduced a modern concurrency model with a new native syntax for asynchronous operations and tighter integration between the concurrent APIs, the compiler and runtime.

Most of the books from raywenderlich.com are "By Tutorials". Since this book targets developers who already have intermediate/advanced Swift skills, however, we skipped that part of the book title.

The book chapters consist of a healthy mix of theory sections that introduce new concepts and APIs, and step-by-step tutorials. If you work through all the projects, by the time you're done, the new concurrency model won't hold any secrets for you!

Take a deep breath and enjoy the ride!

# How to read this book

Most of this book's chapters build from one concept to the next. We suggest reading it chapter-by-chapter to make sure you aren't missing any crucial knowledge you need for any of the advanced chapters.

However, the chapters are also mostly self-contained, so if you feel comfortable with one of the topics, feel free to skip ahead to the next topic in the list.

# Section I: Modern Concurrency in Swift

# Chapter 1: Why Modern Swift Concurrency?

By Marin Todorov

The last time Apple made a big deal about an asynchronous framework was when **Grand Central Dispatch (GCD)** came out, along with Mac OS X Snow Leopard, in 2009.

While GCD helped Swift launch in 2014 with support for concurrency and asynchrony from day one, that support wasn't native — it was designed around the needs and abilities of Objective-C. Swift just "borrowed" that concurrency until it had its own mechanism, designed specifically for the language.

All that changed with Swift 5.5, which introduced a new, native model for writing asynchronous, concurrent code.

The new **concurrency model** provides everything you need to write safe and performant programs in Swift, including:

- A new, native syntax for running asynchronous operations in a structured way.

- A bundle of standard APIs to design asynchronous and concurrent code.

- Low-level changes in the libdispatch framework, which make all the high-level changes integrate directly into the operating system.

- A new level of compiler support for creating safe, concurrent code.

Swift 5.5 introduces the new language syntax and APIs to support these features. In your apps, besides using a recent Swift version, you also need to target certain platform versions:

- If you're using Xcode 13.2 or newer, it will bundle the new concurrency runtime with your app so you can target iOS 13 and macOS 10.15 (for native apps).

- In case you're on Xcode 13 but earlier version than 13.2, you'll be able to target only iOS 15 or macOS 12 (or newer).

In the first chapter of the book, you'll review the new concurrency support in Swift and see how it fares compared to the existing APIs. Later, in the practical part of the chapter, you'll work on a real-life project by trying out the `async`/`await` syntax and adding some cool asynchronous error-handling.

# Understanding asynchronous and concurrent code

Most code runs the same way you see it written in your code editor: from top to bottom, starting at the beginning of your function and progressing line-by-line to the end.

This makes it easy to determine when any given code line executes — it simply follows the one before it. The same is true for function calls: When your code runs **synchronously**, the execution happens sequentially.

In a synchronous context, code runs in one **execution thread** on a single CPU core. You can imagine synchronous functions as cars on a single-lane road, each driving behind the one in front of it. Even if one vehicle has a higher priority, like an ambulance on duty, it cannot "jump over" the rest of the traffic and drive faster.

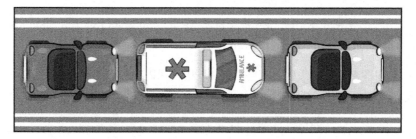

On the other hand, iOS apps and Cocoa-based macOS apps are inherently **asynchronous**.

Asynchronous execution allows different pieces of the program to run in any order on one thread — and, sometimes, *at the same time* on multiple threads, depending on many different events like user input, network connections and more.

In an asynchronous context, it's hard to tell the *exact order* in which functions run, especially when several asynchronous functions need to use the same thread. Just like driving on a road where you have stoplights and places where traffic needs to yield, functions must sometimes wait until it's their turn to continue, or even stop until they get a green light to proceed.

One example of an asynchronous call is making a network request and providing a completion closure to run when the web server responds. While waiting to run the completion callback, the app uses the time to do other chores.

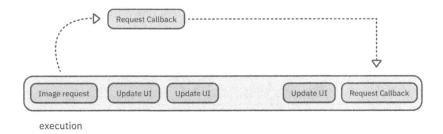

To intentionally run parts of your program **in parallel**, you use **concurrent** APIs. Some APIs support executing a fixed number of tasks at the same time; others start a concurrent group and allow an arbitrary number of concurrent tasks.

This also causes a myriad of concurrency-related problems. For example, different parts of the program might block each other's execution, or you might encounter the much-loathed **data-races**, where two or more functions simultaneously access the same variable, crashing the app or unexpectedly corrupting your app's state.

However, when used with care, concurrency can help your program run faster by executing different functions simultaneously on multiple CPU cores, the same way careful drivers can move much faster on a multi-lane freeway.

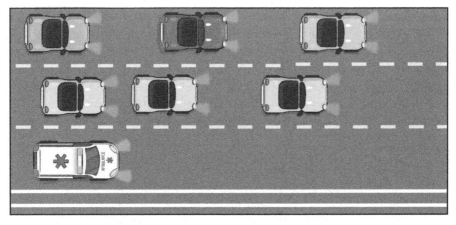

Multiple lanes allow faster cars to go around slower vehicles. Even more importantly, you can keep the emergency lane free for high-priority vehicles, like ambulances or firetrucks.

Similarly, when executing code, high-priority tasks can "jump" the queue before lower-priority tasks, so you avoid blocking the main thread and keep it free for critical updates to the UI.

A real use-case for this is a photo browsing app that needs to download a group of images from a web server *at the same time*, scale them down to thumbnail size and store them in a cache.

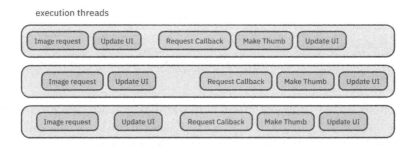

While asynchrony and concurrency both sound great, you might ask yourself: "Why did Swift need a *new* concurrency model?". You've probably worked on apps that used at least some of the features described above in the past.

Next, you'll review the pre-Swift 5.5 concurrency options and learn what's different about the new `async/await` model.

# Reviewing the existing concurrency options

Pre-Swift 5.5, you used GCD to run asynchronous code via dispatch queues — an abstraction over threads. You also used older APIs that are 'closer to the metal', like Operation, Thread or even interacting with the C-based pthread library directly.

> **Note**: You won't use GCD in this book because the new Swift concurrency APIs have replaced it. If you're curious, read Apple's GCD documentation: Dispatch documentation (https://apple.co/3tOlEuO).

Those APIs all use the same foundation: **POSIX threads**, a standardized execution model that doesn't rely on any given programming language. Each execution flow is a **thread**, and multiple threads might overlap and run at the same time, similarly to the multi-lane car example presented above.

Thread wrappers like Operation and Thread require you to **manually manage** execution. In other words, you're responsible for creating and destroying threads, deciding the order of execution for concurrent jobs and synchronizing shared data across threads. This is error-prone and tedious work.

GCD's queue-based model worked well. However, it would often cause issues, like:

- **Thread explosion**: Creating too many concurrent threads requires constantly switching between active threads. This ultimately *slows down* your app.

- **Priority inversion**: When arbitrary, low-priority tasks block the execution of high-priority tasks waiting in the same queue.

- **Lack of execution hierarchy**: Asynchronous code blocks lacked an execution hierarchy, meaning each task was managed independently. This made it difficult to cancel or access running tasks. It also made it complicated for a task to return a result to its caller.

To address these shortcomings, Swift introduced a brand-new concurrency model. Next, you'll see what modern concurrency in Swift is all about!

# Introducing the modern Swift concurrency model

The new concurrency model is tightly integrated with the language syntax, the Swift runtime and Xcode. It abstracts away the notion of threads for the developer. Its key new features include:

1. A cooperative thread pool.

2. `async/await` syntax.

3. Structured concurrency.

4. Context-aware code compilation.

With this high-level overview behind you, you'll now take a deeper look at each of these features.

## 1. A cooperative thread pool

The new model transparently manages a pool of threads to ensure it doesn't exceed the number of CPU cores available. This way, the runtime doesn't need to create and destroy threads or constantly perform expensive thread switching. Instead, your code can suspend and, later on, resume very quickly on any of the available threads in the pool.

## 2. async/await syntax

Swift's new `async/await` syntax lets the compiler and the runtime know that a piece of code might suspend and resume execution one or more times in the future. The runtime handles this for you seamlessly, so you don't have to worry about threads and cores.

As a wonderful bonus, the new language syntax often removes the need to weakly or strongly capture `self` or other variables because you don't need to use escaping closures as callbacks.

# 3. Structured concurrency

Each asynchronous task is now part of a hierarchy, with a parent task and a given priority of execution. This hierarchy allows the runtime to cancel all child tasks when a parent is canceled. Furthermore, it allows the runtime to *wait* for all children to complete before the parent completes. It's a tight ship all around.

This hierarchy provides a huge advantage and a more obvious outcome, where high-priority tasks will run before any low-priority tasks in the hierarchy.

# 4. Context-aware code compilation

The compiler keeps track of whether a given piece of code *could* run asynchronously. If so, it won't let you write potentially unsafe code, like mutating shared state.

This high level of compiler awareness enables elaborate new features like **actors**, which differentiate between synchronous and asynchronous access to their state at compile time and protects against inadvertently corrupting data by making it harder to write unsafe code.

With all those advantages in mind, you'll move on to writing some code with the new concurrency features right away and see how it feels for yourself!

# Running the book server

Throughout the rest of this chapter, you'll create a fully-fledged stock trading app with live price monitoring called **LittleJohn**.

You'll work through the code at a *quick pace*, with a somewhat brief explanation of the APIs. Enjoy the process and don't worry about the mechanics right now. You'll go into the nitty-gritty details at length in the coming chapters.

First things first: Most of the projects in this book need access to a web API to fetch JSON data, download images and more. The book comes with its own server app, called the **book server** for short, that you need to run in the background at all times while working through the chapters.

Open your Mac's Terminal app and navigate to the **00-book-server** folder in the book materials repository. Start the app by entering:

```
swift run
```

The first time you run the server, it will download a few dependencies and build them — which might take a minute or two. You'll know the server is up and running when you see the following message:

```
[ NOTICE ] Server starting on http://127.0.0.1:8080
```

To double-check that you can access the server, launch your favorite web browser and open the following address: http://localhost:8080/hello (http://localhost:8080/hello).

This contacts the book server running on your computer, which will respond with the current date:

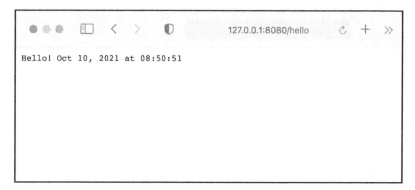

Later, when you've finished working on a given project and want to stop the server, switch to your Terminal window and press **Control-C** to end the server process.

> **Note**: The server itself is a Swift package using the Vapor framework, but this book won't cover that code. If you're curious, you're welcome to open it in Xcode and read through it.

# Getting started with LittleJohn

As with all projects in this book, LittleJohn's SwiftUI views, navigation, and data model are already wired up and ready for you. It's a simple ticker app that displays selected "stock prices" live:

> **Note**: The server sends random numbers to the app. Don't read anything into any upward or downward trends of these fictitious prices!

As mentioned earlier, simply *go with the flow* in this chapter and enjoy working on the app. Don't worry if you don't entirely understand every detail and line of code. You'll revisit everything you do here in later chapters, where you'll learn about all the APIs in greater detail.

The first thing you need to do is to add some asynchronous code to the main app screen.

# Writing your first async/await

As your first task, you'll add a function to the app's model that fetches a list of available stocks from the web server in JSON format. That's a very common task in iOS programming, so it's a fitting first step.

Open the starter version of LittleJohn in this chapter's materials, under **projects/starter**. Then, open **LittleJohnModel.swift** and add a new method inside LittleJohnModel:

```
func availableSymbols() async throws -> [String] {
  guard let url = URL(string: "http://localhost:8080/littlejohn/
symbols")
  else {
    throw "The URL could not be created."
  }
}
```

Woah, those are some major modern-concurrency features right here!

The async keyword in the method's definition lets the compiler know that the code runs in an asynchronous context. In other words, it says that the code might suspend and resume at will. Also, regardless of how long the method takes to complete, it ultimately returns a value much like a synchronous method does.

Next, add the code below to call URLSession and fetch data from the book server:

```
let (data, response) = try await URLSession.shared.data(from:
url)
```

Calling the async method URLSession.data(from:delegate:) suspends availableSymbols() and resumes it when it gets the data back from the server:

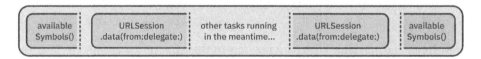

Using await gives the runtime a **suspension point**: a place to *pause* your method, consider if there are other tasks to run first and then continue running your code.

It's *so neat* that you make an asynchronous call but never have to worry about threads or passing closures around!

Next, you need to verify the server response and return the fetched data. Append this code to complete your method:

```
guard (response as? HTTPURLResponse)?.statusCode == 200 else {
  throw "The server responded with an error."
}

return try JSONDecoder().decode([String].self, from: data)
```

First, you check that the response code is 200. In server language, this indicates a successful **OK** response. Then, you try to decode the response data as a list of Strings. If that succeeds, you return the result.

You'll learn about async/await in greater detail in Chapter 2, "Getting Started With async/await".

> **Note**: Web servers can respond with a myriad of status codes; this book won't cover them all. Check out this list if you want to know more: HTTP status codes (https://bit.ly/2YzI2ww).

# Using async/await in SwiftUI

Press **Command-B** to compile the project and verify you correctly added all the code so far, but don't run it just yet. Next, open **SymbolListView.swift**, where you'll find the SwiftUI code for the symbol list screen.

The essential part here is the ForEach that displays the symbols in a list onscreen. You need to call LittleJohnModel.availableSymbols(), which you just created, and assign its result to SymbolListView.symbols to get everything to work together.

Inside SymbolListView.body, find the .padding(.horizontal) view modifier. Add the following code immediately below it:

```
.onAppear {
  try await model.availableSymbols()
}
```

If you're paying attention to Xcode, you'll notice that the method
availableSymbols() is grayed out in the code's autocompletion:

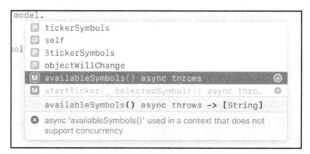

You'll also see the compiler rightfully complain:

```
Invalid conversion from throwing function of type '() async
throws -> Void' to non-throwing function type '() -> Void'
```

Xcode tells you that onAppear(...) runs code synchronously; however, you're
trying to call an asynchronous function in that non-concurrent context.

Luckily, you can use the .task(priority:_:) view modifier instead of
onAppear(...), which will allow you to call asynchronous functions right away.

Remove onAppear(...) and replace it with:

```
.task {
  guard symbols.isEmpty else { return }
}
```

task(priority:_:) allows you to call asynchronous functions but, just like
onAppear(_:), it's called each time the view appears onscreen. That's why you start
by making sure you don't have symbols already.

Now, to call your new async function, append the following inside the task { ... }
modifier:

```
do {
  symbols = try await model.availableSymbols()
} catch {

}
```

As before, you use both try and await to signify that the method might either throw
an error or asynchronously return a value. You assign the result to symbols, and ...
that's all you need to do.

You'll notice the catch portion is still empty. You'll definitely want to handle the erroneous case where availableSymbols can't provide a valid response.

The UI in the starter project has already been wired to display an alert box if you update lastErrorMessage, so you'll use that functionality here. Add the following line inside the empty catch block:

```
lastErrorMessage = error.localizedDescription
```

Swift catches the error, regardless of which thread throws it. You simply write your error handling code as if your code is entirely synchronous. Amazing!

Quickly check that the server is still running in your Terminal, then build and run the app.

As soon as the app launches, you'll briefly see an activity indicator and then a list of stock symbols:

Awesome! Your next task is to test that the asynchronous error handling works as expected. Switch to Terminal and press **Control-C** to stop the book server.

Run your project one more time. Now, your `catch` block will handle the error and assign it to `lastErrorMessage`. Then, the SwiftUI code will pick it up and an alert box will pop up:

Writing modern Swift code isn't that difficult after all, is it?

I get it if you're excited about how few lines you needed here for your networking. To be honest, I'm excited, too; I really needed to restrain myself from ending every sentence with an exclamation mark!

# Using asynchronous sequences

Even though this is just the introduction of this book, you'll still get to try out some more advanced topics — namely, asynchronous sequences.

Asynchronous sequences are similar to the "vanilla" Swift sequences from the standard library. The *hook* of asynchronous sequences is that you can iterate over their elements asynchronously as more and more elements become available over time.

Open **TickerView.swift**. This is a SwiftUI view, similar in structure to `SymbolListView`. It revolves around a `ForEach` that displays stock price changes over time.

In the previous section, you "fired" an async network request, waited for the result, and then returned it. For `TickerView`, that same approach won't work because you can't wait for the request to complete and *only then* display the data. The data needs to keep coming in indefinitely and bring in those price updates.

Here, the server will send you a single long-living response, adding more and more text to it over time. Each text line is a complete JSON array that you can decode on its own:

```
[{"AAPL": 102.86}, {"BABA": 23.43}]
// .. waits a bit ...
[{"AAPL": 103.45}, {"BABA": 23.08}]
// .. waits some more ...
[{"AAPL": 103.67}, {"BABA": 22.10}]
// .. waits even some more ...
[{"AAPL": 104.01}, {"BABA": 22.17}]
// ... continuous indefinitely ...
```

On the live ticker screen, you'll iterate over each line of the response and update the prices onscreen in real time!

In `TickerView`, find `.padding(.horizontal)`. Directly below that line, add a `task` modifier and call the model's method that starts the live price updates:

```
.task {
  do {
    try await model.startTicker(selectedSymbols)
  } catch {
    lastErrorMessage = error.localizedDescription
  }
}
```

The code looks similar to what you did in `SymbolListView`, except that the method doesn't return a result. You'll be handling continuous updates, not a single return value.

Open **LittleJohnModel.swift** and find the `startTicker(_:)` placeholder method, where you'll add your live updates. A published property called `tickerSymbols` is already wired up to the UI in the ticker screen, so updating this property will propagate the changes to your view.

Next, add the following code to the end of `startTicker(_:)`:

```
let (stream, response) = try await liveURLSession.bytes(from:
url)
```

`URLSession.bytes(from:delegate:)` is similar to the API you used in the previous section. However, instead of data, it returns an asynchronous sequence that you can iterate over time. It's assigned to `stream` in your code.

Additionally, instead of using the shared URL session, you use a custom pre-configured session called liveURLSession, which makes requests that never expire or time out. This lets you keep receiving a super-long server response indefinitely.

Just as before, the first thing to do is check for a successful response code. Add the following code at the end of the same function:

```
guard (response as? HTTPURLResponse)?.statusCode == 200 else {
  throw "The server responded with an error."
}
```

Now comes the fun part. Append a new loop:

```
for try await line in stream.lines {

}
```

stream is a sequence of bytes that the server sends as a response. lines is an abstraction of that sequence that gives you that response's lines of text, one by one.

You'll iterate over the lines and decode each one as JSON. To do that, insert the following inside the for loop:

```
let sortedSymbols = try JSONDecoder()
  .decode([Stock].self, from: Data(line.utf8))
  .sorted(by: { $0.name < $1.name })

tickerSymbols = sortedSymbols
```

If the decoder successfully decodes the line as a list of symbols, you sort them and assign them to tickerSymbols to render them onscreen. If the decoding fails, JSONDecoder simply throws an error.

Run the book server again if it's still turned off from your last error handling test. Then, build and run the app. In the first screen, select a few stocks:

Then tap **Live ticker** to see the live price updates on the next screen:

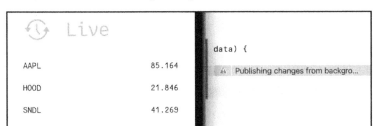

Though you'll most likely see some price updates, you'll also notice glitches and a big purple warning in your code editor saying `Publishing changes from background threads is not allowed....`

# Updating your UI from the main thread

Earlier, you published updates by updating a `@State` property, and SwiftUI took care to route the updates through the main thread. Now, you update `tickerSymbols` from within the same context where you're running your asynchronous work, without specifying that it's a UI update, so the code ends up running on an arbitrary thread in the pool.

This causes SwiftUI some grief because it naturally expects your code to be kosher when it updates the UI.

Luckily, you can switch to the main thread any time you need to. Replace the line `tickerSymbols = sortedSymbols` with the following code:

```
await MainActor.run {
  tickerSymbols = sortedSymbols
  print("Updated: \(Date())")
}
```

`MainActor` is a type that runs code on the main thread. You can easily run any code with it by calling `MainActor.run(_:)`

The extra `print` in there helps you check that your updates come through.

Run the app and go to the live prices screen. This time around, you'll see the prices continuously go up and down:

Hopefully, you enjoyed this first encounter with asynchronous sequences. You'll learn a great deal more about them in Chapter 3, "AsyncSequence & Intermediate Task".

# Canceling tasks in structured concurrency

As mentioned earlier, one of the big leaps for concurrent programming with Swift is that modern, concurrent code executes in a structured way. Tasks run in a strict hierarchy, so the runtime knows who's the parent of a task and which features new tasks should inherit.

For example, look at the `task(_:)` modifier in `TickerView`. Your code calls `startTicker(_:)` asynchronously. In turn, `startTicker(_:)` asynchronously *awaits* `URLSession.bytes(from:delegate:)`, which returns an async sequence that you iterate over:

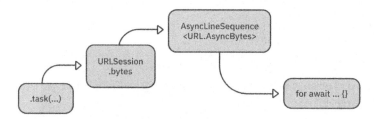

At each suspension point — that is, every time you see the `await` keyword — the thread could potentially change. Since you start the entire process inside `task(_:)`, the async task is the parent of all those other tasks, regardless of their execution thread or suspension state.

The `task(_:)` view modifier in SwiftUI takes care of canceling your asynchronous code when its view goes away. Thanks to structured concurrency, which you'll learn much more about later in this book, all asynchronous tasks are also canceled when the user navigates out of the screen.

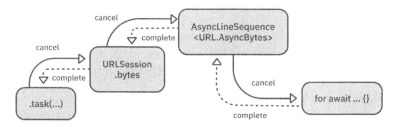

To verify how this works in practice, navigate to the updates screen and look at the Xcode console to check that you see the debug prints from `LittleJohnModel.liveTicker(_:)`:

```
Updated: 2021-08-12 18:24:12 +0000
Updated: 2021-08-12 18:24:13 +0000
Updated: 2021-08-12 18:24:14 +0000
Updated: 2021-08-12 18:24:15 +0000
Updated: 2021-08-12 18:24:16 +0000
Updated: 2021-08-12 18:24:17 +0000
Updated: 2021-08-12 18:24:18 +0000
```

Now, tap **Back**. `TickerView` disappears and the `task(_:)` view modifier's task is canceled. This cancels all child tasks, including the call to `LittleModel.liveTicker(_:)`. As a result, the debug logs in the console stop as well, verifying that all execution ends!

You'll notice, however, an additional message in the console that looks something like:

```
[Presentation] Attempt to present
<SwiftUI.PlatformAlertController: 0x7f8051888000> on ... whose
view is not in the window hierarchy.
```

SwiftUI is logging an issue with your code trying to present an alert after you dismiss the ticker view. This happens because some of the inner tasks throw a cancellation error when the runtime cancels your call to `model.startTicker(selectedSymbols)`.

# Handling cancellation errors

Sometimes you don't care if one of your suspended tasks gets canceled. Other times — like the current situation with that pesky alert box — you'd like to do something special when the runtime cancels a task.

Scroll to the task { ... } modifier in TickerView. Here, you catch all the errors and store their messages for display. However, to avoid the runtime warning in your console, you have to handle cancellation differently than other errors.

Newer asynchronous APIs like Task.sleep(nanoseconds:) throw a CancellationError. Other APIs that throw custom errors have a dedicated cancellation error code, like URLSession.

Replace the catch block with the following code:

```
} catch {
  if let error = error as? URLError,
    error.code == .cancelled {
    return
  }

  lastErrorMessage = error.localizedDescription
}
```

The new catch block checks if the thrown error is a URLError with the cancelled error code. If it is, you return without presenting the message onscreen.

You get a URLError from the ongoing URLSession that fetches the live updates. If you use other modern APIs, they might throw a CancellationError instead.

Run the app one more time and confirm that this last change fixes the behavior and you don't get the runtime warning anymore.

Now, you've finished working on LittleJohn. Congratulations, you completed the first project in this book!

Stick around if you'd like to work through a challenge on your own. Otherwise, turn the page and move on to learning about async/await and Task in more detail!

# Challenges

## Challenge: Adding extra error handling

There's one edge case that the app still doesn't handle graciously: What if the server becomes unavailable while the user is observing the price updates?

You can reproduce this situation by navigating to the prices screen, then stopping the server by pressing **Control-C** in the terminal window.

No error messages pop up in the app because there is no error, per se. In fact, the response sequence simply completes when the server closes it. In this case, your code continues to execute with no error, but it produces no more updates.

In this challenge, you'll add code to reset `LittleJohnModel.tickerSymbols` when the async sequence ends and then navigate out of the updates screen.

In `LittleJohnModel.startTicker(_:)`, after the `for` loop, append code to set `tickerSymbols` to an empty array if the async sequence unexpectedly ends. Don't forget to make this update using `MainActor`.

Next, in `TickerView`, add a new view modifier that observes the number of observed ticker symbols and dismisses the view if the selection resets:

```
.onChange(of: model.tickerSymbols.count) { newValue in
  if newValue == 0 {
    presentationMode.wrappedValue.dismiss()
  }
}
```

Note that the starter already includes an environment `presentationMode` ready to use.

If everything goes well, when you stop the server while watching the live updates in the app, LittleJohn will automatically dismiss the updates screen and go back to the list of symbols.

If you get stuck in the challenge or if something doesn't work as you expect, be sure to check the solution in this chapter's materials.

# Key points

- Swift 5.5 introduces a **new concurrency model** that solves many of the existing concurrency issues, like thread explosion, priority inversion, and loose integration with the language and the runtime.

- The `async` keyword defines a function as asynchronous. `await` lets you wait in a non-blocking fashion for the result of the asynchronous function.

- Use the `task(priority:_:)` view modifier as an `onAppear(_:)` alternative when you want to run asynchronous code.

- You can naturally loop over an asynchronous sequence over time by using a `for try await` loop syntax.

# Chapter 2: Getting Started With async/await

By Marin Todorov

Now that you know what Swift Concurrency is and why you should use it, you'll spend this chapter diving deeper into the actual async/await syntax and how it coordinates asynchronous execution.

You'll also learn about the Task type and how to use it to create new asynchronous execution contexts.

Before that, though, you'll spend a moment learning about pre-Swift 5.5 concurrency as opposed to the new async/await syntax.

## Pre-async/await asynchrony

Up until Swift 5.5, writing asynchronous code had many shortcomings. Take a look at the following example:

```
class API {
  ...
  func fetchServerStatus(completion: @escaping (ServerStatus) ->
Void) {
    URLSession.shared
      .dataTask(
        with: URL(string: "http://amazingserver.com/status")!
      ) { data, response, error in
        // Decoding, error handling, etc
        let serverStatus = ...
        completion(serverStatus)
      }
      .resume()
  }
```

```
  }

class ViewController {
  let api = API()
  let viewModel = ViewModel()

  func viewDidAppear() {
    api.fetchServerStatus { [weak viewModel] status in
      guard let viewModel = viewModel else { return }
      viewModel.serverStatus = status
    }
  }
}
```

This is a short block of code that calls a network API and assigns the result to a property on your view model. It's deceptively simple, yet it exhibits an excruciating amount of ceremony that obscures your intent. Even worse, it creates *a lot* of room for coding errors: Did you forget to check for an error? Did you really invoke the completion closure in every code path?

Since Swift used to rely on Grand Central Dispatch (GCD), a framework designed originally for Objective-C, it couldn't integrate asynchrony tightly into the language design from the get-go. Objective-C itself only introduced blocks (the parallel of a Swift closure) in iOS 4.0, years after the inception of the language.

Take a moment to inspect the code above. You might notice that:

- The compiler has no clear way of knowing how many times you'll call completion inside fetchServerStatus(). Therefore, it can't optimize its lifespan and memory usage.

- You need to handle memory management yourself by weakly capturing viewModel, then checking in the code to see if it was released before the closure runs.

- The compiler has no way to make sure you handled the error. In fact, if you forget to handle error in the closure, or don't invoke completion altogether, the method will silently freeze.

- And the list goes on and on...

The modern concurrency model in Swift works closely with both the compiler *and* the runtime. It solves many issues, including those mentioned above.

The modern concurrency model provides the following three tools to achieve the same goals as the example above:

- **async**: Indicates that a method or function is asynchronous. Using it lets you *suspend* execution until an asynchronous method returns a result.

- **await**: Indicates that your code might pause its execution while it waits for an async-annotated method or function to return.

- **Task**: A unit of asynchronous work. You can wait for a task to complete or cancel it before it finishes.

Here's what happens when you rewrite the code above using the modern concurrency features introduced in Swift 5.5:

```swift
class API {
  ...
  func fetchServerStatus() async throws -> ServerStatus {
    let (data, _) = try await URLSession.shared.data(
      from: URL(string: "http://amazingserver.com/status")!
    )
    return ServerStatus(data: data)
  }
}

class ViewController {
  let api = API()
  let viewModel = ViewModel()

  func viewDidAppear() {
    Task {
      viewModel.serverStatus = try await api.fetchServerStatus()
    }
  }
}
```

The code above has about the same number of lines as the earlier example, but the intent is clearer to both the compiler and the runtime. Specifically:

- **fetchServerStatus()** is an asynchronous function that can suspend and resume execution. You mark it by using the async keyword.

- **fetchServerStatus()** either returns Data or throws an error. This is checked at compile time — no more worrying about forgetting to handle an erroneous code path!

- **Task** executes the given closure in an asynchronous context so the compiler knows what code is safe (or unsafe) to write in that closure.

- Finally, you give the runtime an opportunity to suspend or cancel your code every time you call an asynchronous function by using the **await** keyword. This lets the system constantly change the priorities in the current task queue.

# Separating code into partial tasks

Above, you saw that "the code might suspend at each `await`" — but what does that mean? To optimize shared resources such as CPU cores and memory, Swift *splits up* your code into logical units called **partial tasks**, or **partials**. These represent parts of the code you'd like to run asynchronously.

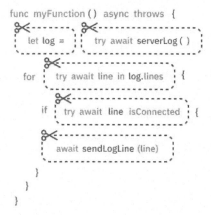

The Swift runtime schedules each of these pieces separately for asynchronous execution. When each partial task completes, the system decides whether to continue with your code or to execute another task, depending on the system's load and the priorities of the pending tasks.

That's why it's important to remember that each of these `await`-annotated partial tasks might run on a different thread at the system's discretion. Not only can the thread change, but you shouldn't make assumptions about the app's state after an `await`; although two lines of code appear one after another, they might execute some time apart. Awaiting takes an arbitrary amount of time, and the app state might change significantly in the meantime.

To recap, `async/await` is a simple syntax that packs a lot of punch. It lets the compiler guide you in writing safe and solid code, while the runtime optimizes for a well-coordinated use of shared system resources.

# Executing partial tasks

As opposed to the closure syntax mentioned at the beginning of this chapter, the modern concurrency syntax is light on ceremony. The keywords you use, such as `async`, `await` and `let`, clearly express your intent. The foundation of the concurrency model revolves around breaking asynchronous code into partial tasks that you execute on an **Executor**.

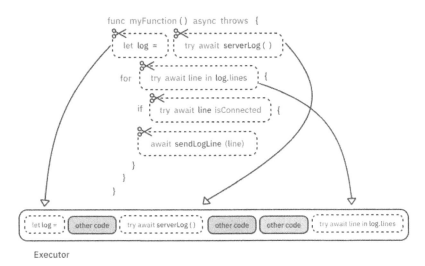

Executors are similar to GCD queues, but they're more powerful and lower-level. Additionally, they can quickly run tasks and completely hide complexity like order of execution, thread management and more.

# Controlling a task's lifetime

One essential new feature of modern concurrency is the system's ability to manage the lifetime of the asynchronous code.

A huge shortcoming of existing multi-threaded APIs is that once an asynchronous piece of code starts executing, the system cannot graciously reclaim the CPU core until the code decides to give up control. This means that even after a piece of work is no longer needed, it still consumes resources and performs its work for no real reason.

A good example of this is a service that fetches content from a remote server. If you call this service twice, the system doesn't have any automatic mechanism to reclaim resources that the first, now-unneeded call used, which is an unnecessary waste of resources.

The new model breaks your code into partials, providing suspension points where you check in with the runtime. This gives the system the opportunity to not only suspend your code but to **cancel it** altogether, at its discretion.

Thanks to the new asynchronous model, when you cancel a given task, the runtime can walk down the async hierarchy and cancel all the child tasks as well.

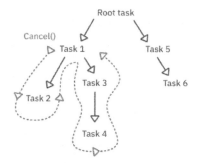

But what if you have a hard-working task performing long, tedious computations without any suspension points? For such cases, Swift provides APIs to detect if the current task has been canceled. If so, you can manually give up its execution.

Finally, the suspension points also offer an **escape route** for errors to bubble up the hierarchy to the code that catches and handles them.

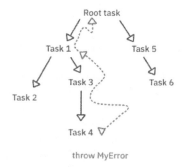

The new model provides an error-handling infrastructure similar to the one that synchronous functions have, using modern and well-known **throwing functions**. It also optimizes for quick memory release as soon as a task throws an error.

You already see that the recurring topics in the modern Swift concurrency model are safety, optimized resource usage and minimal syntax. Throughout the rest of this chapter, you'll learn about these new APIs in detail and try them out for yourself.

# Getting started

**SuperStorage** is an app that lets you browse files you've stored in the cloud and download them for local, on-device preview. It offers three different "subscription plans", each with its own download options: "Silver", "Gold" and "Cloud 9".

Open the starter version of SuperStorage in this chapter's materials, under **projects/ starter**.

Like all projects in this book, **SuperStorage**'s SwiftUI views, navigation and data model are already wired up and ready to go. This app has more UI code compared to **LittleJohn**, which you worked on in the previous chapter, but it provides more opportunities to get your hand dirty with some asynchronous work.

> **Note**: The server returns mock data for you to work with; it is not, in fact, a working cloud solution. It also lets you reproduce slow downloads and erroneous scenarios, so don't mind the download speed. There's nothing wrong with your machine.

While working on SuperStorage in this and the next chapter, you'll create async functions, design some concurrent code, use async sequences and more.

## A bird's eye view of async/await

async/await has a few different flavors depending on what you intend to do:

- To declare a function as asynchronous, add the async keyword before throws or the return type. Call the function by prepending await and, if the function is throwing, try as well. Here's an example:

```
func myFunction() async throws -> String {
  ...
}

let myVar = try await myFunction()
```

- To make a computed property asynchronous, simply add async to the getter and access the value by prepending await, like so:

```
var myProperty: String {
  get async {
    ...
  }
}

print(await myProperty)
```

- For closures, add `async` to the signature:

```
func myFunction(worker: (Int) async -> Int) -> Int {
  ...
}

myFunction {
  return await computeNumbers($0)
}
```

Now that you've had a quick overview of the `async/await` syntax, it's time to try it for yourself.

# Getting the list of files from the server

Your first task is to add a method to the app's model that fetches a list of available files from the web server in JSON format. This task is almost identical to what you did in the previous chapter, but you'll cover the code in more detail.

Open **SuperStorageModel.swift** and add a new method anywhere inside `SuperStorageModel`:

```
func availableFiles() async throws -> [DownloadFile] {
  guard let url = URL(string: "http://localhost:8080/files/
list") else {
    throw "Could not create the URL."
  }
}
```

Don't worry about the compiler error Xcode shows; you'll finish this method's body momentarily.

You annotate the method with `async throws` to make it a **throwing, asynchronous function**. This tells the compiler and the Swift runtime how you plan to use it:

- The compiler makes sure you don't call this function from synchronous contexts where the function can't suspend and resume the task.

- The runtime uses the new cooperative thread pool to schedule and execute the method's partial tasks.

In the method, you fetch a list of decodable `DownloadFiles` from a given `url`. Each `DownloadedFile` represents one file available in the user's cloud.

# Making the server request

At the end of the method's body, add this code to execute the server request:

```
let (data, response) = try await
  URLSession.shared.data(from: url)
```

You use the shared URLSession to asynchronously fetch the data from the given URL. It's vital that you do this asynchronously because doing so lets the system use the thread to do other work while it waits for a response. It doesn't block others from using the shared system resources.

Each time you see the await keyword, think **suspension point**. await means the following:

- The current code will suspend execution.

- The method you await will execute either immediately or later, depending on the system load. If there are other pending tasks with higher priority, it might need to wait.

- If the method or one of its child tasks throws an error, that error will bubble up the call hierarchy to the nearest catch statement.

Using await funnels each and every asynchronous call through the central dispatch system in the runtime, which:

- Prioritizes jobs.

- Propagates cancellation.

- Bubbles up errors.

- And more.

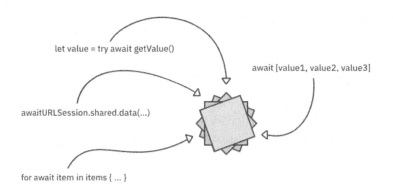

# Verifying the response status

Once the asynchronous call completes successfully and returns the server response data, you can verify the response status and decode the data as usual. Add the following code at the end of `availableFiles()`:

```
guard (response as? HTTPURLResponse)?.statusCode == 200 else {
  throw "The server responded with an error."
}

guard let list = try? JSONDecoder()
  .decode([DownloadFile].self, from: data) else {
  throw "The server response was not recognized."
}
```

You first inspect the response's HTTP status code to confirm it's indeed **HTTP 200 OK**. Then, you use a `JSONDecoder` to decode the raw `Data` response to an array of `DownloadFiles`.

# Returning the list of files

Once you decode the JSON into a list of `DownloadFile` values, you need to return it as the asynchronous result of your function. How simple is it to do that? Very.

Simply add the following line to the end of `availableFiles()`:

```
return list
```

While the execution of the method is entirely *asynchronous*, the code reads entirely *synchronously* which makes it relatively easy to maintain, read through and reason about.

# Displaying the list

You can now use this new method to feed the file list on the app's main screen. Open **ListView.swift** and add one more view modifier directly after .alert(...), near the bottom of the file:

```
.task {
  guard files.isEmpty else { return }

  do {
    files = try await model.availableFiles()
  } catch {
    lastErrorMessage = error.localizedDescription
  }
}
```

As mentioned in the previous chapter, task is a view modifier that allows you to execute asynchronous code when the view appears. It also handles canceling the asynchronous execution when the view disappears.

In the code above, you:

1. Check if you already fetched the file list; if not, you call availableFiles() to do that.

2. Catch and store any errors in lastErrorMessage. The app will then display the error message in an alert box.

# Testing the error handling

If the book server is still running from the previous chapter, stop it. Then, build and run the project. Your code inside .task(...) will catch a networking error, like so:

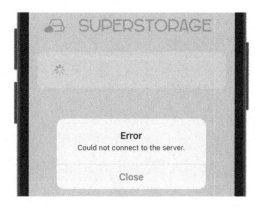

Asynchronous functions propagate errors up the call hierarchy, just like synchronous Swift code. If you ever wrote Swift code with asynchronous error handling before async/await's arrival, you're undoubtedly ecstatic about the new way to handle errors.

## Viewing the file list

Now, start the book server. If you haven't already done that, navigate to the server folder **00-book-server** in the book materials-repository and enter swift run. The detailed steps are covered in Chapter 1, "Why Modern Swift Concurrency?".

Restart the SuperStorage app and you'll see a list of files:

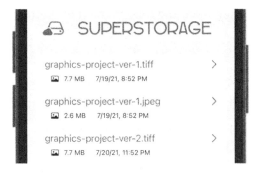

Notice there are a few TIFF and JPEG images in the list. These two image formats will give you various file sizes to play with from within the app.

## Getting the server status

Next, you'll add one more asynchronous function to the app's model to fetch the server's status and get the user's usage quota.

Open **SuperStorageModel.swift** and add the following method to the class:

```
func status() async throws -> String {
  guard let url = URL(string: "http://localhost:8080/files/
status") else {
    throw "Could not create the URL."
  }
}
```

A successful server response returns the status as a text message, so your new function asynchronously returns a String as well.

As you did before, add the code to asynchronously get the response data and verify the status code:

```
let (data, response) = try await
  URLSession.shared.data(from: url, delegate: nil)

guard (response as? HTTPURLResponse)?.statusCode == 200 else {
  throw "The server responded with an error."
}
```

Finally, decode the response and return the result:

```
return String(decoding: data, as: UTF8.self)
```

The new method is now complete and follows the same pattern as `availableFiles()`.

## Showing the service status

For your next task, you'll use `status()` to show the server status in the file list.

Open **ListView.swift** and add this code inside the `.task(...)` view modifier, after assigning `files`:

```
status = try await model.status()
```

Build and run. You'll see some server usage data at the bottom of the file list:

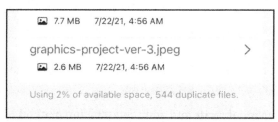

Everything works great so far, but there's a hidden optimization opportunity you might have missed. Can you guess what it is? Move on to the next section for the answer.

# Grouping asynchronous calls

Revisit the code currently inside the `task` modifier:

```
files = try await model.availableFiles()
status = try await model.status()
```

Both calls are asynchronous and, in theory, could happen at the same time. However, by explicitly marking them with `await`, the call to `status()` doesn't start until the call to `availableFiles()` completes.

Sometimes, you need to perform sequential asynchronous calls — like when you want to use data from the first call as a parameter of the second call.

This isn't the case here, though!

For all you care, both server calls can be made *at the same time* because they don't depend on each other. But how can you await *both* calls without them blocking each other? Swift solves this problem with a feature called **structured concurrency**, via the `async let` syntax.

## Using async let

Swift offers a special syntax that lets you group several asynchronous calls and await them all together.

Remove all the code inside the `task` modifier and use the special `async let` syntax to run two concurrent requests to the server:

```
guard files.isEmpty else { return }

do {
  async let files = try model.availableFiles()
  async let status = try model.status()
} catch {
  lastErrorMessage = error.localizedDescription
}
```

An `async let` binding allows you to create a local constant that's similar to the concept of promises in other languages. **Option-Click** `files` to bring up Quick Help:

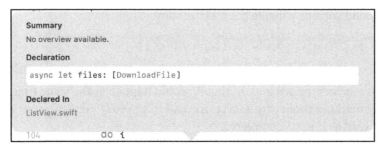

The declaration explicitly includes `async let`, which means you can't access the value without an `await`.

The `files` and `status` bindings promise that either the values of the specific types or an error will be available later.

To read the binding results, you need to use `await`. If the value is already available, you'll get it immediately. Otherwise, your code will suspend at the `await` until the result becomes available:

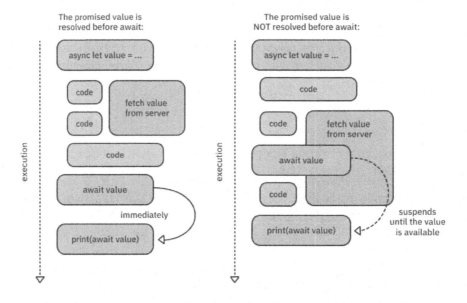

> **Note**: An `async let` binding feels similar to a promise in other languages, but in Swift, the syntax integrates much more tightly with the runtime. It's not just syntactic sugar but a feature implemented into the language.

# Extracting values from the two requests

Looking at the last piece of code you added, there's a *small detail* you need to pay attention to: The async code in the two calls starts executing right away, *before* you call `await`. So `status` and `availableFiles` run in parallel to your main code, inside the `task` modifier.

To group concurrent bindings and extract their values, you have two options:

- Group them in a collection, such as an array.

- Wrap them in parentheses as a tuple and then destructure the result.

The two syntaxes are interchangeable. Since you have only two bindings, you'll use the tuple syntax here.

Add this code at the end of the do block:

```
let (filesResult, statusResult) = try await (files, status)
```

And what are `filesResult` and `statusResult`? **Option-Click** `filesResults` to check for yourself:

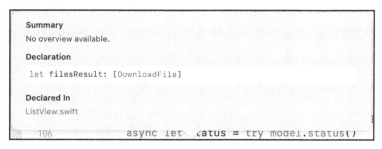

This time, the declaration is simply a `let` constant, which indicates that by the time you can access `filesResult` and `statusResult`, both requests have finished their work and provided you with a final result.

At this point in the code, if an `await` didn't throw in the meantime, you know that all the concurrent bindings resolved successfully.

## Updating the view

Now that you have both the file list and the server status, you can update the view. Add the following two lines at the end of the do block:

```
self.files = filesResult
self.status = statusResult
```

Build and run. This time, you execute the server requests in parallel, and the UI becomes ready for the user a little faster than before.

Take a moment to appreciate that the same async, await and let syntax lets you run non-blocking asynchronous code serially and *also* in parallel. That's some amazing API design right there!

# Asynchronously downloading a file

Open **SuperStorageModel.swift** and scroll to the method called download(file:). The starter code in this method creates the endpoint URL for downloading files. It returns empty data to make the starter project compile successfully.

SuperStorageModel includes two methods to manage the current app downloads:

- **addDownload(name:)**: Adds a new file to the list of ongoing downloads.

- **updateDownload(name:progress:)**: Updates the given file's progress.

You'll use these two methods to update the model and the UI.

## Downloading the data

To perform the actual download, add the following code directly before the return line in download(file:):

```
addDownload(name: file.name)

let (data, response) = try await
  URLSession.shared.data(from: url, delegate: nil)

updateDownload(name: file.name, progress: 1.0)
```

`addDownload(name:)` adds the file to the published `downloads` property of the model class. `DownloadView` uses it to display the ongoing download statuses onscreen.

Then, you fetch the file from the server. Finally, you update the progress to `1.0` to indicate the download finished.

## Adding server error handling

To handle any possible server errors, also append the following code before the `return` statement:

```
guard (response as? HTTPURLResponse)?.statusCode == 200 else {
  throw "The server responded with an error."
}
```

Finally, replace `return Data()` with:

```
return data
```

Admittedly, emitting progress updates here is not very useful because you jump from 0% directly to 100%. However, you'll improve this in the next chapter for the premium subscription plans — Gold and Cloud 9.

For now, open **DownloadView.swift**. Scroll to the code that instantiates the file details view, `FileDetails(...)`, then find the closure parameter called `downloadSingleAction`.

This is the action for the leftmost button — the cheapest download plan in the app.

So far, you've only used `.task()` in SwiftUI code to run async calls. But how would you await `download(file:)` inside the `downloadSingleAction` closure, which doesn't accept async code?

Add this inside the closure to double-check that the closure expects synchronous code:

```
fileData = try await model.download(file: file)
```

```
a single   ⊗  Invalid conversion from throwing function of type '() async throws -> ()' to non-throwing function type   ⊗
model.down:     '() -> Void'
```

The error states that your code is asynchronous — it's of type `() async throws -> Void` — but the parameter expects a synchronous closure of type `() -> Void`.

One viable solution is to change `FileDetails` to accept an asynchronous closure. But what if you don't have access to the source code of the API you want to use? Fortunately, there is another way.

# Running async requests from a non-async context

While still in **DownloadView.swift**, replace `fileData = try await model.download(file: file)` with:

```
Task {
  fileData = try await model.download(file: file)
}
```

It seems like the compiler is happy with this syntax! But wait, what is this `Task` type you used here?

# A quick detour through Task

`Task` is a type that represents a **top-level asynchronous task**. Being top-level means it can *create* an asynchronous context — which can start from a synchronous context.

Long story short, any time you want to run asynchronous code from a synchronous context, you need a new `Task`.

You can use the following APIs to manually control a task's execution:

- **Task(priority:operation)**: Schedules `operation` for asynchronous execution with the given priority. It inherits defaults from the current synchronous context.

- **Task.detached(priority:operation)**: Similar to `Task(priority:operation)`, except that it doesn't inherit the defaults of the calling context.

- **Task.value**: Waits for the task to complete, then returns its value, similarly to a promise in other languages.

- **Task.isCancelled**: Returns `true` if the task was canceled since the last suspension point. You can inspect this boolean to know when you should stop the execution of scheduled work.

- **Task.checkCancellation()**: Throws a `CancellationError` if the task is canceled. This lets the function use the error-handling infrastructure to yield execution.

- **Task.sleep(nanoseconds:)**: Makes the task sleep for at least the given number of nanoseconds, but doesn't block the thread while that happens.

In the previous section, you used `Task(priority:operation:)`, which created a new asynchronous task with the `operation` closure and the given `priority`. By default, the task inherits its priority from the current context — so you can usually omit it.

You need to specify a priority, for example, when you'd like to create a low-priority task from a high-priority context or vice versa.

Don't worry if this seems like a lot of options. You'll try out many of these throughout the book, but for now, let's get back to the SuperStorage app.

## Creating a new task on a different actor

In the scenario above, `Task` runs on the actor that called it. To create the same task without it being a part of the actor, use `Task.detached(priority:operation:)`.

> **Note**: Don't worry if you don't know what actors are yet. This chapter mentions them briefly because they're a core concept of modern concurrency in Swift. You'll dig deeper into actors later in this book.

For now, remember that when your code creates a Task from the main thread, that task will run on the main thread, too. Therefore, you know you can update the app's UI safely.

Build and run one more time. Select one of the JPEG files and tap the **Silver plan** download button. You'll see a progress bar and, ultimately, a preview of the image.

However, you'll notice that the progress bar glitches and sometimes only fills up halfway. That's a hint that you're updating the UI from a background thread.

And just as in the previous chapter, there's a log message in Xcode's console and a friendly purple warning in the code editor:

```
class SuperStorageModel: ObservableObject {
  /// The list of currently running downloads.
  @Published var downloads = [DownloadInfo]()   ⚠  Publishing changes from background
}
```

But why? You create your new async Task from your UI code on the main thread — and now *this* happens!

Remember, you learned that every use of await is a suspension point, and your code might resume on a different thread. The first piece of your code runs on the main thread because the task initially runs on the main actor. But after the first await, your code can execute on *any* thread.

You need to **explicitly** route any UI-driving code back to the main thread.

# Routing code to the main thread

One way to ensure your code is on the main thread is calling `MainActor.run()`, as you did in the previous chapter. The call looks something like this (no need to add this to your code):

```
await MainActor.run {
  ... your UI code ...
}
```

`MainActor` is a type that runs code on the main thread. It's the modern alternative to the well-known `DispatchQueue.main`, which you might have used in the past.

While it gets the job done, using `MainActor.run()` too often results in code with many closures, making it hard to read. A more elegant solution is to use the `@MainActor` annotation, which lets you automatically route calls to given functions or properties to the main thread.

## Using @MainActor

In this chapter, you'll annotate the two methods that update `downloads` to make sure those changes happen on the main UI thread.

Open **SuperStorageModel.swift** and prepend @MainActor to the definition of `addDownload(file:)`:

```
@MainActor func addDownload(name: String)
```

Do the same for `updateDownload(name:progress:)`:

```
@MainActor func updateDownload(name: String, progress: Double)
```

Any calls to those two methods will automatically run on the main actor — and, therefore, on the main thread.

# Running the methods asynchronously

Offloading the two methods to a specific actor (the main actor or any other actor) requires that you call them asynchronously, which gives the runtime a chance to suspend and resume your call on the correct actor.

Scroll to download(file:) and fix the two compile errors.

Replace the synchronous call to addDownload(name: file.name) with:

```
await addDownload(name: file.name)
```

Then, prepend await when calling updateDownload:

```
await updateDownload(name: file.name, progress: 1.0)
```

That clears up the compile errors. Build and run. This time, the UI updates smoothly with no runtime warnings.

> **Note**: To save space on your machine, the server always returns the same image.

# Updating the download screen's progress

Before you wrap up this chapter, there's one loose end to take care of. If you navigate back to the file list and select a different file, the download screen keeps displaying the progress from your previous download.

You can fix this quickly by resetting the model in onDisappear(...). Open **DownloadView.swift** and add one more modifier to body, just below toolbar(...):

```
.onDisappear {
  fileData = nil
  model.reset()
}
```

In here, you reset the file data and invoke reset() on the model too, which clears the download list.

That's it, you can now preview multiple files one after the other, and the app keeps behaving.

# Challenges

## Challenge: Displaying a progress view while downloading

In DownloadView, there's a state property called isDownloadActive. When you set this property to true, the file details view displays an activity indicator next to the filename.

For this challenge, your goal is to show the activity indicator when the file download starts and hide it again when the download ends.

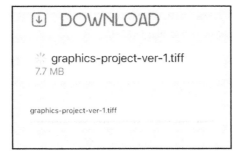

Be sure to also hide the indicator when the download throws an error. Check the **projects/challenges** folder for this chapter in the chapter materials to compare your solution with the suggested one.

# Key points

- Functions, computed properties and closures marked with **async** run in an asynchronous context. They can suspend and resume one or more times.

- **await** *yields* the execution to the central async handler, which decides which pending job to execute next.

- An **async let** binding promises to provide a value or an error later on. You access its result using `await`.

- **Task()** creates an asynchronous context for running on the current actor. It also lets you define the task's priority.

- Similar to `DispatchQueue.main`, **MainActor** is a type that executes blocks of code, functions or properties on the main thread.

This chapter gave you a deeper understanding of how you can create, run and wait for asynchronous tasks and results using the new Swift concurrency model and the async/await syntax.

You might've noticed that you only dealt with asynchronous pieces of work that yield a *single* result. In the next chapter, you'll learn about `AsyncSequence`, which can emit multiple results for an asynchronous piece of work. See you there!

# Chapter 3: AsyncSequence & Intermediate Task

By Marin Todorov

Throughout this book, you'll use async sequences to make your life easier when it comes to asynchronous programming. Async sequences make consuming asynchronous results as simple as iterating over a Swift sequence.

You've already tried async sequences briefly in Chapter 1, "Why Modern Swift Concurrency?", but you'll take a more detailed deep dive into them now.

You'll do this while continuing to work on the **SuperStorage** app from the last chapter, so you don't need an introduction to the project; you can jump right in. When you've finished working through this chapter, you'll have given SuperStorage parallel download superpowers.

# Getting to know AsyncSequence

**AsyncSequence** is a protocol describing a sequence that can produce elements **asynchronously**. Its surface API is identical to the Swift standard library's Sequence, with one difference: You need to await the next element, since it might not be immediately available, as it would in a regular Sequence

Here are some common tasks you'd use an asynchronous sequence for:

- Iterating over the sequence in a for loop, using await and, if the AsyncSequence is throwing, try. The code suspends **at each loop iteration** to get the next value:

```
for try await item in asyncSequence {
  // Next item from `asyncSequence`
}
```

- Using the asynchronous alternative of a standard library iterator with a while loop. This is similar to using a synchronous sequence: You need to make an iterator and repeatedly call next() using await until the sequence is over:

```
var iterator = asyncSequence.makeAsyncIterator()
while let item = try await iterator.next() {
  ...
}
```

- Using standard sequence methods like dropFirst(_:), prefix(_:) and filter(_:):

```
for await item in asyncSequence
  .dropFirst(5)
  .prefix(10)
  .filter { $0 > 10 }
  .map { "Item: \($0)" } {
    ...
  }
```

- Using special raw-byte sequence wrappers, such as for file contents or when fetching from a server URL:

```
let bytes = URL(fileURLWithPath: "myFile.txt").resourceBytes

for await character in bytes.characters {
  ...
}

for await line in bytes.lines {
  ...
}
```

- Creating custom sequences by adopting `AsyncSequence` in your own types.

- Finally, you can create your very own custom async sequences by leveraging `AsyncStream`. You'll learn all about this option in the next chapter.

For an overview of all the Apple-provided types that are asynchronous sequences, visit `AsyncSequence`'s online documentation (https://apple.co/3AS4Tkw). You'll find the available types listed under **Conforming Types**.

# Getting started with AsyncSequence

So far, you've done good work on the **SuperStorage** app including building the main screen, which displays a list of files. When the user selects a file, they see its details with three download options, one for each of the cloud service's subscription plans:

In the previous chapter, you coded the **Silver** download option, which fetches the complete file in one go and presents an onscreen preview.

You'll start this chapter by implementing the **Gold** download option, which provides progressive UI updates as the file downloads.

You'll achieve this by reading the file as an asynchronous sequence of bytes from the server. This lets you update the progress bar as you receive the file's contents.

## Adding your asynchronous sequence

Open the **SuperStorage** project and go to **SuperStorageModel.swift**, scrolling to downloadWithProgress(fileName:name:size:offset:). It already contains code to create the correct server URL. It also calls addDownload(name:) to add the download onscreen.

Next, insert this code before downloadWithProgress(fileName:name:size:offset:)'s return line:

```
let result: (downloadStream: URLSession.AsyncBytes, response:
URLResponse)
```

Unlike before, when you used URLSession.data(for:delegate:) to return Data, you'll use an alternative API that returns URLSession.AsyncBytes. This sequence gives you the bytes it receives from the URL request, asynchronously.

The HTTP protocol lets a server define that it supports a capability called **partial requests**. If the server supports it, you can ask it to return a **byte range** of the response, instead of the entire response at once. To make things a little more interesting, you'll support both standard and partial requests in the app.

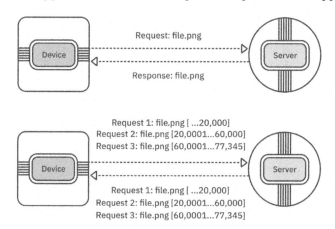

Using partial response functionality lets you split the file into parts and download them in parallel. You'll need this functionality when implementing the **Cloud 9** download option later in this chapter.

Continue by adding the code below to make a partial file request:

```
if let offset = offset {
  let urlRequest = URLRequest(url: url, offset: offset, length:
size)
  result = try await
    URLSession.shared.bytes(for: urlRequest, delegate: nil)

  guard (result.response as? HTTPURLResponse)?.statusCode == 206
else {
    throw "The server responded with an error."
  }
}
```

If the code specifies an `offset`, you create a URL request and pass it to `URLSession.bytes(for:delegate:)`, which returns a tuple of the response details and an async sequence that enumerates the bytes of the file.

This time, you check if the response code is **206**, indicating a successful partial response.

Next, append the following `else` block, which handles a regular, non-partial request, to complete your `if` statement:

```
else {
  result = try await URLSession.shared.bytes(from: url,
delegate: nil)

  guard (result.response as? HTTPURLResponse)?.statusCode == 200
else {
    throw "The server responded with an error."
  }
}
```

The code above is similar to what you did previously except that, this time, you're checking for a 200 status and a successful server response.

Regardless of whether you make a partial or standard request, you end up with an asynchronous byte sequence available in `result.downloadStream`.

# Using ByteAccumulator

Now, it's time to start iterating over the response bytes. In this chapter, you'll implement custom logic to iterate over the bytes. You'll use a type called ByteAccumulator, which is included with the starter project, to fetch batches of bytes from the sequence.

Why do you need to process the file in batches? Not only is it more fun, but a file can contain millions or billions of bytes. You don't want to update the UI after getting each byte.

ByteAccumulator will help you collect all of the file's contents and update the UI only periodically, after fetching each batch of bytes:

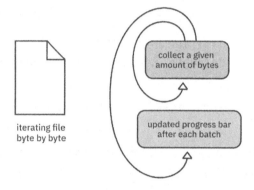

iterating file
byte by byte

collect a given
amount of bytes

updated progress bar
after each batch

> **Note**: If you're curious to see how the accumulator works, peek into **ByteAccumulator.swift**.

To start using ByteAccumulator, append this code before the return statement for downloadWithProgress(fileName:name:size:offset:) in SuperStorageModel:

```
var asyncDownloadIterator =
result.downloadStream.makeAsyncIterator()
```

AsyncSequence features a method called makeAsyncIterator(), which returns an asynchronous iterator for the sequence. You'll use the returned asyncDownloadIterator to iterate over the bytes, one at a time.

Now, to add the accumulator and collect all the bytes, add the code that creates and uses the accumulator:

```
let accumulator = ByteAccumulator(name: name, size: size)

while !stopDownloads, !accumulator.checkCompleted() {

}
```

The first condition in the `while` loop checks if the model's `stopDownloads` flag isn't set. You'll use this flag again in a bit.

The second condition checks if `checkCompleted()` returns `false`, which means the accumulator can still collect more bytes.

The combination of these two conditions gives you the flexibility to run the loop until either the external flag `stopDownloads` is lifted or the accumulator completes the download. With this design, you're looking ahead and making the download code easily cancellable by using an external flag, if needed.

Next, insert the following code *inside* the `while` body:

```
while !accumulator.isBatchCompleted,
  let byte = try await asyncDownloadIterator.next() {
  accumulator.append(byte)
}
```

You use a second `while` loop that runs until the particular batch is full. The loop condition is similar to the outer `while` — you keep collecting bytes until either the `isBatchCompleted` flag is `true` or the byte sequence completes.

The code is so simple that if it weren't for the single `await` keyword in there, you couldn't tell it's asynchronously processing a file while downloading it at the same time.

# Updating the progress bar

After a batch completes, the execution continues after the `while` loop. This is the perfect place to update the download progress bar. Insert the following code after the inner `while` loop, still inside `batch`'s trailing closure:

```
Task.detached(priority: .medium) { [weak self] in
  await self?
    .updateDownload(name: name, progress: accumulator.progress)
}

print(accumulator.description)
```

In the code above, you might spot at least a couple of novelties that you haven't covered yet.

First, you use `Task.detached(...)`. This is the *rogue* version of creating a task with `Task(priority:operation:)`. A detached task doesn't inherit the parent's priority, task storage or execution actor.

> **Note**: Generally speaking, the documentation recommends against using `Task.detached(...)` because it negatively affects the concurrency model's efficiency. In this case, however, there's nothing wrong with using it to see how it works.

You create the task with a medium priority, so there's no chance of it slowing down the ongoing download task.

Another interesting aspect is that you weakly capture `self` in the closure. Earlier, you learned that the new syntax mostly obliterates the need to manage memory manually. However, `SuperStorageModel` is a class — and, therefore, a reference type. That means the usual memory management rules apply when you use escaping closures, as you do here.

Secondly, you use `await` with the optional `self?.updateDownload(...)` — and that *just works*, like it does when you await non-optional values.

Last but not least, you print the current accumulator state to the output console so you can keep track of downloads during development.

To make sure you inserted the code in the right places, you'll find the completed loop code below, so you can compare your code to it:

```
while !stopDownloads, !accumulator.checkCompleted() {
  while !accumulator.isBatchCompleted,
    let byte = try await asyncDownloadIterator.next() {
    accumulator.append(byte)
  }
  Task.detached(priority: .medium) { [weak self] in
    await self?
      .updateDownload(name: name, progress:
accumulator.progress)
  }
  print(accumulator.description)
}
```

# Returning the accumulated result

To wrap up the the method you worked on in the last sections, replace the line `return Data()` with:

```
return accumulator.data
```

The newly completed method iterates over the download sequence and collects all the bytes. It then updates the file progress at the end of each batch.

Switch to **DownloadView.swift** and scroll to the closure parameter called downloadWithUpdatesAction. Insert this code inside the empty closure:

```
isDownloadActive = true
Task {
  do {
    fileData = try await model.downloadWithProgress(file: file)
  } catch { }
  isDownloadActive = false
}
```

The code above is identical to the code you added to downloadSingleAction in the previous chapter. This time, however, it calls downloadWithProgress(file:) to provide real-time updates to the progress bar.

This project interacts with the book-server web API. Before testing your code in the iOS Simulator, make sure you're running the server app on your computer. To start the server, navigate to the server folder in the book materials-repository and enter `swift run`. The detailed steps are covered in more detail in Chapter 1, "Why Modern Swift Concurrency?".

Build and run. Select a file and tap the **Gold** option to test your new code. You'll see the progress bar update repeatedly as the file downloads:

Even more reassuring is the console output that the `while` loop prints after each batch:

```
[graphics-project-ver-1.jpeg] 0.9 MB
[graphics-project-ver-1.jpeg] 1 MB
[graphics-project-ver-1.jpeg] 1.2 MB
[graphics-project-ver-1.jpeg] 1.3 MB
[graphics-project-ver-1.jpeg] 1.4 MB
[graphics-project-ver-1.jpeg] 1.6 MB
...
```

This output tells you at what point in the download you're updating the progress bar, and you can easily calculate the size of each batch.

Congratulations, you now know most of what you need to know about using `AsyncSequence`!

# Canceling tasks

Canceling unneeded tasks is essential for the concurrency model to work efficiently.

When you use one of the new APIs, like TaskGroup (which you'll cover later in the book) or async let, the system can usually cancel the task automatically when needed.

You can, however, implement a finer-grained cancellation strategy for your task-based code by using the following Task APIs:

- **Task.isCancelled**: Returns true if the task is still alive but has been canceled since the last suspension point.

- **Task.currentPriority**: Returns the current task's priority.

- **Task.cancel()**: Attempts to cancel the task and its child tasks.

- **Task.checkCancellation()**: Throws a CancellationError if the task is canceled, making it easier to exit a throwing context.

- **Task.yield()**: Suspends the execution of the current task, giving the system a chance to cancel it automatically to execute some other task with higher priority.

When writing your asynchronous tasks, you'll choose which APIs to use depending on whether you need a throwing function like checkCancellation() or if you'd like to manage the control flow yourself by checking isCancelled.

In the next section, you'll implement your own custom cancellation logic using isCancelled.

# Canceling an async task

To demonstrate why canceling tasks in a timely manner is important, run through the following scenario in the app:

Select one of the TIFF files and tap **Gold** to start a download with progress updates. Logs will appear in Xcode's console as the accumulator collects more and more of the file's content.

While the file is still downloading, tap the **< Back** button and observe the console. That download keeps going until it downloads the whole file!

# Manually canceling tasks

So far, you wrote your async code inside a .task(...) view modifier, which is responsible for automatically canceling your code when the view disappears. But the actions for the download buttons *aren't* in a .task(), so there's nothing to cancel your async operations.

To fix this issue, you'll manually cancel your download tasks. Start by adding a new state property to DownloadView:

```
@State var downloadTask: Task<Void, Error>?
```

In downloadTask, you'll store an asynchronous task that returns no result and could throw an error. Task is a type like any other, so you can also store it in your view, model or any other scope. Task doesn't return anything if it's successful, so success is Void; likewise you return an Error if there's a failure.

Next, scroll back to downloadWithUpdatesAction and replace the line Task { with:

```
downloadTask = Task {
```

This stores the task in downloadTask so you can access it later. Most importantly, it lets you cancel the task at will.

You'll cancel the task when the user navigates back to the main screen. You already have some code in .onDisappear(...). Add this line immediately after model.reset():

```
downloadTask?.cancel()
```

Canceling downloadTask will also cancel all its child tasks — and all of their children, and so forth.

Build and run the app. Then, try to run the test scenario from above. You'll notice that the progress logs in the console stop when you navigate back to the main screen.

# Storing state in tasks

Each asynchronous task executes in its own context, which consists of its priority, actor and more. But don't forget — a task can call other tasks. Because each might interact with many different functions, isolating shared data at runtime can be difficult.

To address this, Swift offers a new property wrapper that marks a given property as **task-local**.

Think for a moment about injecting an object into the environment in SwiftUI, which makes the object available not only to the immediate View, but also to all of its child views.

Similarly, binding a task-local value makes it available not only to the immediate task, but also to all its child tasks:

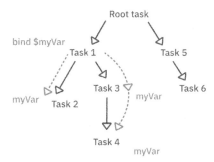

In this section of the chapter, you'll learn how to use task-local storage to make a function's behavior vary depending on the calling context.

More specifically, you'll code the action for the **Cancel All** button on the download screen.

# Adding a partial image preview

The JPEG format allows for partially decoding images, but other formats, such as TIFF, don't allow for partial preview. So you'll only support partial preview for JPEG files.

You'll develop the following custom logic: If the user is downloading a JPEG image and cancels before it finishes, you'll show the partially downloaded preview. For other image types, you'll just abort the download.

Open **SuperStorageModel.swift** and add a new property to SuperStorageModel:

```
@TaskLocal static var supportsPartialDownloads = false
```

If the user initiates a JPEG download, you'll set supportsPartialDownloads to true. You'll then add some new code in SuperStorageModel to provide the appropriate behavior based on the flag's value.

> **Note**: Task-local properties need to be either static for the type, or global variables.

The @TaskLocal property wrapper offers a method called withValue() that allows you to **bind a value** to an async task — or, simply speaking, **inject** it into the task hierarchy.

Open **DownloadView.swift**. In the downloadWithUpdatesAction closure parameter, replace the line fileData = try await model.downloadWithProgress(file: file) with these lines:

```
try await SuperStorageModel
  .$supportsPartialDownloads
  .withValue(file.name.hasSuffix(".jpeg")) {
    fileData = try await model.downloadWithProgress(file: file)
  }
```

Here, you use withValue(_:) to bind whether or not the download supports partial downloads, based on the file's extension. With the value bound, you call downloadWithProgress(file:).

You can bind multiple values this way, and you can also overwrite the values from inner bindings, like so (don't enter this code):

```
try await $property1.withValue(myData) {
  ...
  try await $property2.withValue(myConfig1) {
    ...
    try await serverRequest()
    try await $property2.withValue(myConfig2) {
      ...
    }
  }
}
```

In any case, you can see that using too many task-local storage properties might become difficult to read and reason about since you'll need to wrap the code in a closure for each binding.

> **Note**: In that sense, task storage is useful for binding fewer values: complete configuration objects or whole data models, rather than separate single values or flags as in the example above.

## Adding the "Cancel All" functionality

While still in **DownloadView.swift**, scroll down toward the bottom of the file and find `.toolbar(...)`. This is where you define the **Cancel All** button. Its `action` closure is empty, so add the following code inside:

```
model.stopDownloads = true
```

This time, instead of canceling the download task altogether, like you did in `.onDisappear(...)`, you turn on the `stopDownloads` flag on `SuperStorageModel`. You'll observe this flag while downloading. If it changes to `true`, you'll know that you need to cancel your tasks internally.

To do that, open **SuperStorageModel.swift** and scroll to
`downloadWithProgress(fileName:name:size:offset:)`. Toward the bottom of
that function, insert this code just before the `return` line:

```
if stopDownloads, !Self.supportsPartialDownloads {
  throw CancellationError()
}
```

This is the task-specific behavior for your custom cancellation. After each
downloaded batch, you check if `stopDownloads` is `true` and, if so, also check whether
the download supports partial preview.

Then:

- If `Self.supportsPartialDownloads` is `false`, you throw a `CancellationError`
  to exit the function with an error. This stops the download immediately.

- If `Self.supportsPartialDownloads` is `true`, you continue the execution and
  return the partially downloaded file content.

It's time to give that new feature a try. Build and run. Select a TIFF image, then start
a **Gold** plan download. After a moment, tap **Cancel All**.

As you can see, the download stops. Your existing error-handling code catches the
`CancellationError` and hides the spinner view without further updating the
progress bar.

Now, try picking a JPEG image and running through the same routine:

Here, your *special* behavior for JPEG files returns the partially downloaded image, while `DownloadView` displays a preview of the successfully downloaded part.

# Bridging Combine and AsyncSequence

Combine is Apple's reactive programming framework, based on the reactive streams specification. Its syntax is similar to RxSwift and other frameworks based on or inspired by the Rx standard. You can learn more about Combine by working through the book Combine: Asynchronous Programming With Swift (https:// www.raywenderlich.com/books/combine-asynchronous-programming-with-swift).

Apple has integrated Combine into several key frameworks like Foundation and Core Data, among others:

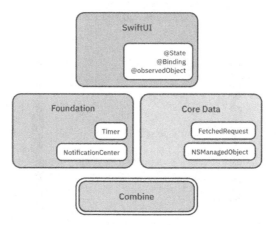

The simplicity of the `Publisher` protocol, which is the cornerstone of Combine, makes it universal and easy to adopt. A publisher can asynchronously emit zero, one or more values. It can, optionally, complete with a success or a failure:

*Wait a minute!*

That looks more or less precisely like an async sequence. Wouldn't it be fantastic if you could use `async/await` with all the existing Combine integrations from Apple, as well as with your own Combine code?

Yes, it would! And, fortunately, Apple offers an easy interface to do just that.

# Adding a progress timer

In this section of the chapter, you'll add a timer showing how long the user's download is taking in real time:

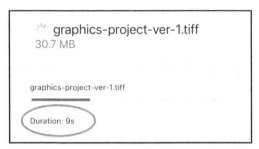

As usual, the starter project already includes the necessary UI code. `DownloadView` has a state property called `duration` that displays the duration below the progress bar.

The plan for the timer is to create a new async task whenever `isDownloadActive` changes to `true` and, in that task, create a Combine timer to update the UI periodically.

First, since you're using Combine, add one more import line at the top of **DownloadView.swift**:

```
import Combine
```

Then, add a new property in `DownloadedView` to store the timer task so you can cancel it when you're done:

```
@State var timerTask: Task<Void, Error>?
```

Next, find the property `@State var isDownloadActive = false`. The first thing you'd like to do when this flag is set to `true` or `false` is to cancel any previously running timer task. Add the following `didSet` accessor to `downloadTask`, so it looks like so:

```
@State var downloadTask: Task<Void, Error>? {
  didSet {
    timerTask?.cancel()
  }
}
```

Then, if the user just started a new download, you want to note the start time. Add this code next, still inside the didSet accessor:

```
guard isDownloadActive else { return }
let startTime = Date().timeIntervalSince1970
```

You'll use this later to calculate the duration based on the timer's start time.

## Creating the Combine-based timer

It's time to create the Combine timer and use the asynchronous values property to proxy your Combine code so you can use it with await.

Add this code to create a Timer publisher immediately after setting startTime:

```
let timerSequence = Timer
  .publish(every: 1, tolerance: 1, on: .main, in: .common)
  .autoconnect()
  .map { date -> String in
    let duration = Int(date.timeIntervalSince1970 - startTime)
    return "\(duration)s"
  }
  .values
```

Here's what this code is doing, step-by-step:

1. Timer.publish creates a Combine publisher that emits the current date every second.

2. autoconnect makes the publisher start ticking automatically whenever someone subscribes to it.

3. map calculates the elapsed time in seconds and returns the duration as a String.

4. Finally, and most importantly, values returns an *asynchronous sequence* of the publisher's events, which you can loop over as usual.

In fact, you can use for await with **any** Combine publisher by accessing its values property, which automatically wraps the publisher in an AsyncSequence.

> **Note**: Similarly, the Future type in Combine offers an async property called value. This lets you await the future result asynchronously.

# Completing the timer

Finally, still in the `didSet` accessor, add this code to create a new asynchronous task, store it in `timerTask` and loop over the sequence:

```
timerTask = Task {
  for await duration in timerSequence {
    self.duration = duration
  }
}
```

Here, you iterate over `timerSequence`. Inside that loop, you assign each value to `self.duration`. As mentioned in the beginning of the section, `duration` is already wired to the UI, so the only thing left to do is test it.

Build and run. Select a file and choose the **Gold** download button. You'll see that the duration summary appears below the progress bar and updates every second.

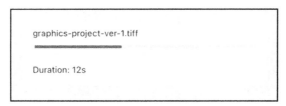

Before wrapping up this chapter, there's one final easy-to-miss issue: Tap **Cancel All**, and you'll notice the timer is still running.

To fix this, scroll down to the `toolbar` modifier and add the following line to the Button's `action` closure:

```
timerTask?.cancel()
```

This will cancel the pending timer whenever you tap the **Cancel All** button. That's it!

By completing the last task for this chapter, you've really become an async sequence pro user. If you're hungry for more practice, however, stay around and work through this chapter's challenge.

# Challenges

## Challenge: Implementing concurrent downloads for the "Cloud 9" plan

To try creating local structured concurrency on your own, your challenge is to implement the **Cloud 9** download option. Don't worry, the starter project already comes with all the non-concurrency code, letting you focus on the essential bits and pieces.

First, head to **DownloadView.swift** and, inside the downloadMultipleAction closure parameter, add a call to multiDownloadWithProgress(file:) on your model. This is just like what you did for the other download buttons.

Once you do that, head to **SuperStorageModel.swift** and find multiDownloadWithProgress(file:).

You'll see that the function already includes code to break the file download into four parts and store them in the parts array. Each array element has the following properties:

- **name**: The part name.

- **size**: The part size in bytes.

- **offset**: The part's offset within the complete file.

Luckily, these are also the exact parameters that downloadWithProgress(fileName:name:size:offset) expects, so putting the pieces together shouldn't be too difficult.

On your own, you should:

1. Define four promises with async let that each use downloadWithProgress(fileName:name:size:offset) to download a part of the file. Use the data in parts.

2. Await all four downloads together to execute them concurrently.

3. Combine the data from all the downloads to return the complete file content as the return value of multiDownloadWithProgress(file:).

Once you've done all of the above, verify that tapping the **Cloud 9** button kicks off four simultaneous downloads, like so:

The most telling sign that everything works as expected will be that the image preview appears correctly at the end of the download:

If you get stuck or want to compare your solution with what I had in mind for this code, look at the completed challenge project in this chapter's materials.

# Key points

- AsyncSequence is a protocol which resembles Sequence and allows you to iterate over a sequence of values asynchronously.

- You iterate over a sequence asynchronously by using the for await ... in syntax, or directly creating an AsyncIterator and awaiting its next() method in the context of a while loop.

- Task offers several APIs to check if the current task was canceled. If you want to throw an error upon cancellation, use Task.checkCancellation(). To safely check and implement custom cancellation logic, use Task.isCancelled.

- To bind a value to a task and all its children, use the @TaskLocal property wrapper along with withValue().

Earlier in this chapter, you learned there are a few ways to create your very own custom asynchronous sequence. Now, equipped with your newly earned mastery of leveraging existing asynchronous sequences, it seems like the perfect time to take a deep dive into AsyncStream, which lets you succinctly create your own asynchronous streams. You'll also learn everything there is to know about the underlying protocols and interesting implementation details that power custom sequences. See you in the next chapter!

# Chapter 4: Custom Asynchronous Sequences With AsyncStream

By Marin Todorov

In previous chapters, you've learned a few different ways to integrate asynchronous code in your apps. By now, you're hopefully comfortable calling and writing `async` functions and iterating over asynchronous sequences.

In this chapter, you'll dive deeper into how to create your very own custom async sequences using `AsyncStream`. Using this method grants you complete control over the asynchronous sequence and makes it trivial to wrap your own existing asynchronous APIs as async sequences.

In this chapter, you'll work through the **Blabber** app to explore these topics.

## Getting started with the Blabber app

**Blabber** is a messaging app that lets you chat with friends. It has some neat features like location sharing, a countdown timer and a friendly — but somewhat unpredictable — chatbot.

Like all projects in this book, Blabber's SwiftUI views, navigation and data model are already wired up and ready for you. Blabber has a similar foundation to the projects you've already worked on, like LittleJohn and SuperStorage. It's a connected app powered by a server API. Some of that code is already included in the starter because it works the same as in earlier projects.

Open the starter version of Blabber in this chapter's materials, under **projects/ starter**. When you complete the app, it will feature a working login screen, where you can choose your user name, and a chat screen to socialize with friends:

At the moment, you can enter a user name, but nothing else works. Your goal is to make asynchronous calls to the server, then provide live updates in the app by reading from a long-living server request.

Before starting to work on the app, start the book server. If you haven't already done that, navigate to the server folder **00-book-server** in the book materials-repository and enter `swift run`. The detailed steps are covered in Chapter 1, "Why Modern Swift Concurrency?".

## Adding functionality to Blabber

In the first section of this chapter, you'll work on finishing some missing app functionality. That will give you a solid start when you work on your own custom sequences in the following sections.

Go to **BlabberModel.swift**, where you'll add most of the app's logic throughout this and the following chapters.

The `chat()` method in `BlabberModel` includes the code to open a long-living request that will return real-time updates.

> **Note**: Just as in previous chapters, "long-living" means the URL request doesn't time out. This lets you keep it open so you can constantly receive server updates in real time.

Once it establishes a connection, that method calls `readMessages(stream:)`. This is the method you'll work on in this section.

# Parsing the server responses

The custom chat protocol that the book server implements sends a status as the first line, then continues with chat messages on the following lines. Each line is a JSON object, and new lines appear whenever users add chat messages. This is all part of the same long-living request/response. Here's an example:

```
{"activeUsers": 4}
...
{"id": "...", "message": "Mr Anderson connected", "date": "..."}
...
{"id": "...", "user": "Mr Anderson", "message": "Knock
knock...", "date": "..."}
/// and so on ...
```

This is a bit different from what you've done in previous chapters — it requires more work to handle the response.

Scroll down to `readMessages(stream:)` and add this code to read the first line of the server response:

```
var iterator = stream.lines.makeAsyncIterator()

guard let first = try await iterator.next() else {
  throw "No response from server"
}
```

In the code above, you first create an iterator over the `lines` sequence of the response. Remember, the server sends each piece of data on a separate text line. You then wait for the first line of the response using `next()`.

> **Note**: Using an iterator and `next()` instead of a `for await` loop lets you be explicit about the number of items you expect to deal with. In this case, you initially expect one, and only one, server status.

Next, decode that server status by adding:

```
guard let data = first.data(using: .utf8),
      let status = try? JSONDecoder()
        .decode(ServerStatus.self, from: data) else {
  throw "Invalid response from server"
}
```

Here, you convert the text line to `Data` and then try to decode it to a `ServerStatus`. The starter project includes a `ServerStatus` data model containing a single property called `activeUsers`. This is how the server tells you how many users are in the chat at the moment.

## Storing and using the chat information

To store this information, add the following code immediately after the decoding:

```
messages.append(
  Message(
    message: "\(status.activeUsers) active users"
  )
)
```

`messages` is a published property on `BlabberModel` that contains the messages displayed onscreen. Most `Message` values are user messages posted in chat. They contain a specific user and date, but in this case, you use a convenience initializer that only accepts the message, as the initial status is considered a **system message**.

To use the server status you fetched, you create a new system message that says **X active users** and add it to the messages array.

After the initial status, the server sends an ever-growing list of chat messages, each on its own line.

This is similar to what you've done in previous chapters. You can abandon the iterator that you just used because the number of items you are expecting is now open-ended.

Next, move on to consuming the rest of the stream with a `for await` loop:

```
for try await line in stream.lines {
  if let data = line.data(using: .utf8),
    let update = try? JSONDecoder().decode(Message.self, from:
data) {
    messages.append(update)
  }
}
```

You iterate over each response line and try to decode it as a `Message`. If the decoding succeeds, you add the new message to `messages`. Just like before, your UI will immediately reflect the change.

Now, the final piece of the app's core is in place. Build and run. Give Blabber a try by entering a user name and tapping the enter button on the right-hand side of the login screen:

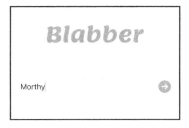

The app reads the first message from the server, then displays the server status at the top of the chat screen. Enter one or more messages in the text field at the bottom, then send them off to the server. You'll see them pop right back onscreen, meaning the server received them and then sent them back to you:

Don't be alarmed if some unexpected messages appear too, as in the screenshot above. This is just the chat bot Bottley trying to jump into the discussion.

When you get bored of talking to Bottley, who isn't the best conversationalist, you can launch more simulators and start a conversation between your alter egos, instead:

Well, look at that — you already have a somewhat functioning chat app at your fingertips. How cool!

# Digging into AsyncSequence, AsyncIteratorProtocol and AsyncStream

In the previous section, you learned that an asynchronous sequence lets you access its elements via its iterator. In fact, defining the element type of the sequence and providing an iterator are the *only* requirements of the AsyncSequence protocol:

```
protocol AsyncSequence {
  ...
  func makeAsyncIterator() -> Self.AsyncIterator
}
```

There are no further requirements regarding *how* you produce the elements, no constraints on the type lifetime — nothing. In fact, quite the opposite: Open AsyncSequence's documentation (https://developer.apple.com/documentation/swift/asyncsequence); you'll see that the protocol comes with a long list of methods, similar to those offered by Sequence:

```
func contains(_:) -> Bool
func allSatisfy(_:) -> Bool
func first(where:) -> Self.Element?
func min() -> Self.Element?
func max() -> Self.Element?
...
```

The iterator also powers for await loops, which you're probably already quite familiar with at this point.

You don't need to limit yourself to the most obvious use cases. Here are just a few examples of different sequences that you might easily create on your own:

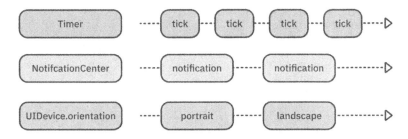

By adopting AsyncSequence, you can take advantage of the default implementations of the protocol, for free: prefix(while:), contains(), min(), max() and so on.

The sequence's iterator must conform to `AsyncIteratorProtocol`, which is also very minimal. It has only one requirement — an `async` method that returns the next element in the sequence:

```
protocol AsyncIteratorProtocol {
  ...
  func next() async throws -> Self.Element?
}
```

# Simple async sequences

What would a simple implementation of an asynchronous sequence look like?

Below is an example of a typewriter — an asynchronous sequence that "types" a phrase adding a character every second. Don't add this code to the project; just review it:

```
struct Typewriter: AsyncSequence {
  typealias Element = String

  let phrase: String

  func makeAsyncIterator() -> TypewriterIterator {
    return TypewriterIterator(phrase)
  }
}
```

The type has a `phrase` to type out, which you pass to the iterator. The iterator looks like this:

```
struct TypewriterIterator: AsyncIteratorProtocol {
  typealias Element = String

  let phrase: String
  var index: String.Index

  init(_ phrase: String) {
    self.phrase = phrase
    self.index = phrase.startIndex
  }

  mutating func next() async throws -> String? {
    guard index < phrase.endIndex else {
      return nil
    }
    try await Task.sleep(nanoseconds: 1_000_000_000)
    defer {
      index = phrase.index(after: index)
```

```
    }
    return String(phrase[phrase.startIndex...index])
  }
}
```

The iterator holds a copy of the string. Each time you call next(), it returns a substring of the initial string that is one character longer than the last one.

Finally, when it reaches the end of the phrase, either by a for await loop or some code that calls next() directly, next() returns nil to signify the end of the sequence.

**Note**: If you're wondering why Task.sleep(nanoseconds:) is throwing — it throws a CancellationError if the current task is canceled while it's sleeping. Throwing an error is the quickest way to cleanly and safely wrap up the current execution without waiting the given amount of time.

You can now use this type like any other AsyncSequence:

```
for try await item in Typewriter(phrase: "Hello, world!") {
  print(item)
}
```

Which produces the following output, eventually:

```
H
He
Hel
Hell
Hello
Hello,
Hello,
Hello, w
Hello, wo
Hello, wor
Hello, worl
Hello, world
Hello, world!
```

As easy as creating a custom `AsyncSequence` is, it still requires you to add two extra types to your codebase.

To avoid clutter, you can make a single type conform to both `AsyncSequence` and `AsyncIteratorProtocol`, but there's also another, *much* easier, way.

# Simplifying async sequences with AsyncStream

To streamline creating asynchronous sequences, Apple has added a type called `AsyncStream`, which aims to make creating async sequences as simple and quick as possible.

It conforms to `AsyncSequence` and produces values from a single closure, where you define the custom logic for your sequence.

This is a big win for decreasing complexity in your code, because you don't have to add additional types every time you need a new asynchronous sequence.

`AsyncStream` has a minimal interface, other than inheriting all the default methods from `AsyncSequence`:

- **init(_:bufferingPolicy:_:)**: Creates a new stream that produces values of the given type, by the given closure. Your closure can control the sequence via a structure called a **continuation**. Produced but unconsumed values are held in a buffer. If you don't use the option to set storage limits for that buffer, all the unconsumed values will be buffered.

- **init(unfolding:onCancel:)**: Creates a new stream that produces values by returning them from the `unfolding` closure. It optionally executes an `onCancel` closure when it's canceled.

To reproduce the typewriter example using `AsyncStream`, you'd write code like this:

```
var phrase = "Hello, world!"
var index = phrase.startIndex
let stream = AsyncStream<String> {
  guard index < phrase.endIndex else { return nil }
  do {
    try await Task.sleep(nanoseconds: 1_000_000_000)
  } catch {
    return nil
  }

  defer { index = phrase.index(after: index) }
  return String(phrase[phrase.startIndex...index])
}
```

```
for try await item in stream {
  print(item)
}
```

This code uses the unfolding variant of AsyncStream, where the closure just returns the next value in the sequence.

Now that you see how AsyncStream works, you'll use its continuation variant to implement the countdown feature in Blabber.

# Creating an asynchronous timer with AsyncStream

The countdown feature in the Blabber app adds an element of drama to your chats by counting down before showing your latest message. You'll use AsyncStream and Timer to achieve this.

Open **BlabberModel.swift** and scroll to countdown(to:). The timer button in the UI calls this method when the user taps it. Right now, it's empty and ready for you to add some code.

Add this code at the bottom of the method:

```
let counter = AsyncStream<String> { continuation in

}
```

This creates an AsyncStream that produces String values. Inside the trailing closure, you'll add your own logic to produce those values.

Note the continuation argument — this lets you control the sequence. continuation is of type AsyncStream.Continuation and offers methods to produce values, error out or complete the sequence. You'll use all of those options shortly.

Your countdown sequence doesn't do very much. It starts at three and counts down to one before finally terminating with the user's message:

# Building your timer logic

Now, it's time to start building the timer's logic. Insert this *inside* AsyncStream's trailing closure:

```
var countdown = 3
Timer.scheduledTimer(
  withTimeInterval: 1.0,
  repeats: true
) { timer in

}
```

Here, you initialize your counter variable, countdown, with the initial value of 3 and create a Timer that fires each second.

Now, insert this code *inside* the Timer's closure:

```
continuation.yield("\(countdown) ...")
countdown -= 1
```

On every timer tick, you call yield(_:) on the  continuation to produce a value, then decrease the counter. You'll add the code to stop the timer when you reach zero in a moment.

Build and run. Once you log in, enter something in the text field and tap the timer button:

Nothing happens! Right now, your stream is producing values, but nobody's listening. The values will buffer until something consumes them:

To iterate over the values, add this code at the bottom of the method, outside any of the previous closures:

```
for await countdownMessage in counter {
  try await say(countdownMessage)
}
```

You call say(_:) for each of the values, which sends all the messages over to the server.

Build and run one more time. Go through the same routine: Log in, enter a message and tap the timer button. The stream starts producing values, and your for await loop gets one of them every second:

The asynchronous stream is practically ready! You still need to stop the counter when it reaches zero and send the user's message.

## Stopping the timer and sending the message

Move back to the Timer's closure in scheduledTimer(...) and insert the following at the top, before the code yielding the values:

```
guard countdown > 0 else {
  timer.invalidate()
  continuation.yield("🎉 " + message)
  continuation.finish()
  return
}
```

This code:

- Stops the timer when the counter reaches zero.

- Yields a final value: the user's initial message.

- Finally, calls `continuation.finish()` to complete the sequence.

You often need to produce the last value *and* complete the sequence at the same time. Fortunately, there's a shortcut for that. Replace the two method calls you just added on `continuation` with:

```
continuation.yield(with: .success(" " + message))
```

This produces the last sequence value and finishes it in a single call.

To make sure you entered all the closure code correctly, here's the completed `AsyncStream` code:

```
let counter = AsyncStream<String> { continuation in
  var countdown = 3
  Timer.scheduledTimer(
    withTimeInterval: 1.0,
    repeats: true
  ) { timer in
    guard countdown > 0 else {
      timer.invalidate()
      continuation.yield(with: .success(" " + message))
      return
    }

    continuation.yield("\(countdown) ...")
    countdown -= 1
  }
}
```

Build and run. Play through the timer routine and you'll see the completed message sequence:

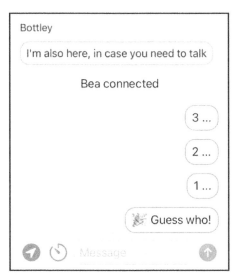

With your new timer messages feature, you're on your way to building the chat client of the future! Or at least, knowing how to do so properly. :]

Next, you'll learn how to wrap existing closure-based asynchronous APIs as async sequences.

# Adding an asynchronous stream to NotificationCenter

Going back and forth between closure-based asynchronous APIs and the modern `async/await`-based APIs can be tedious. Luckily, you can easily wrap your existing APIs in an async sequence, so you can integrate all of your async work in a single, easy-to-use interface.

In this section of the chapter, you'll try your hand at converting another system-provided API into an asynchronous sequence. Specifically, you'll add a method to `NotificatonCenter` that lets you iterate over notifications in a `for await` loop:

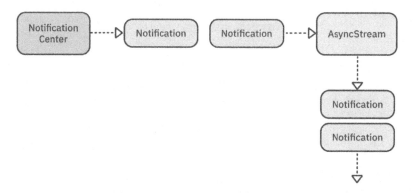

You'll use your new, asynchronous API to send messages like **user went away** and **user came back** to the server when the user closes or re-opens the app.

> **Note**: Since writing this chapter, Apple added a built-in API to observe notifications asynchronously called `NotificationCenter.notifications(named:object:)`. Notifications remain, regardless, a great way for you to learn about wrapping synchronous APIs.

Open **Utility/NotificationCenter+.swift**. Inside, an empty extension declaration waits for you to add your new method to it.

Add the following:

```
func notifications(for name: Notification.Name) ->
AsyncStream<Notification> {
  AsyncStream<Notification> { continuation in

  }
}
```

This method takes a notification name and returns an iterable, asynchronous stream.

Next, you'll observe the required notifications and use `yield(_:)` to add them to the stream.

Insert this code **inside** AsyncStream's closure:

```
NotificationCenter.default.addObserver(
  forName: name,
  object: nil,
  queue: nil
) { notification in
  continuation.yield(notification)
}
```

Here, you observe the default center for notifications with the given name. Whenever one comes in, you pipe it through via continuation.yield(_:). A notification stream is infinite, because there isn't a fixed number of notifications.

Now, open **BlabberModel.swift** and add a new method to observe the app status and post updates to the server:

```
func observeAppStatus() async {

}
```

Inside the method, add a for await loop to iterate over willResignActiveNotification notifications:

```
for await _ in await NotificationCenter.default
  .notifications(for:
UIApplication.willResignActiveNotification) {

}
```

The system posts that notification when you switch to a different app or go back to your device's home screen and the current app isn't active anymore. Note how you use _ in the loop assignment because you aren't interested in the notification's details.

# Notifying participants when a user leaves

To post a system message that the user has left the chat, add the following inside the loop you added at the end of the previous section:

```
try? await say("\(username) went away", isSystemMessage: true)
```

You call say(_:) as before, except you set the isSystemMessage to true. Because this is an automated message, you ignore any errors thrown from here.

Now, call observeAppStatus() just before you start the updates from the chat server. Scroll to readMessages(stream:) and insert this code *before* the for await loop:

```
let notifications = Task {
  await observeAppStatus()
}
```

This creates a new asynchronous task and starts observing for notifications. You store that task in the local notifications variable because — as you might have guessed already — you want to cancel the observation once the loop completes.

Immediately after the last few lines, add this code:

```
defer {
  notifications.cancel()
}
```

This will cancel your observation safely because the code in defer will run when either the for await loop throws or it completes successfully.

With that out of the way, it's time to test the notification sequence! Build and run. Log in, then:

1.  Go to the home screen by clicking **Device ▸ Home** in the iOS Simulator menu or pressing **Command-Shift-H**.

2.  Click **Device ▸ App Switcher** in the menu, then click **Blabber** to go back to the app. You can also simply find the Blabber icon on the simulator's home screen and tap it to go back to the app.

You'll see the **X went away** message on all connected simulators:

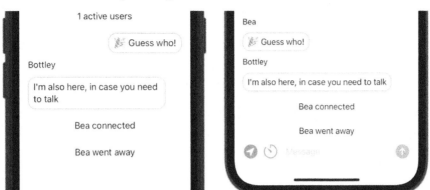

Now that you've notified your participants when a user leaves, it's time to let them know when users come back as well.

## Notifying participants when a user returns

To wrap up this section, you'll also observe `didBecomeActiveNotification` to let the chat participants know when a user returns to the chat.

Scroll to `observeAppStatus()` and find the spot to add a second loop to observe for the additional notification.

Should you add the second `for await` loop *before* or *after* the first one? Since the code execution suspends for the duration of the loop, you can't do *either* — because one of the two loops will then have to wait for the other to complete.

The two loops need to run in parallel, so you have to wrap each one in a `Task`. Edit `observeAppStatus()` to run the two tasks in parallel, like so:

```
func observeAppStatus() async {
  Task {
    for await _ in await NotificationCenter.default
      .notifications(for:
UIApplication.willResignActiveNotification) {
      try? await say("\(username) went away", isSystemMessage:
true)
    }
  }

  Task {
    for await _ in await NotificationCenter.default
      .notifications(for:
UIApplication.didBecomeActiveNotification) {
```

```
        try? await say("\(username) came back", isSystemMessage:
  true)
      }
    }
}
```

Build and run one more time. Repeat the same test routine as the last time. Your code handles both notifications and there are two system messages, one for when you leave the app and another when you come back:

# Extending AsyncSequence

Extending existing types is not an async/await feature per se, but with AsyncStream being so simple to use, your attention might stray away from the possibilities of extending the concrete AsyncStream type or even the more generic AsyncSequence protocol.

In this section, you'll add a new method to AsyncSequence to make iterating over sequences more readable in some cases.

The Swift Sequence protocol features a handy convenience method called forEach(_:) that runs the given closure for each of the sequence's elements. You'll add the same method to AsyncSequence so you can use forEach(_:) instead of the for await loop.

`forEach(_:)` comes in handy when your code uses multiple sequence methods in succession to process the elements, like so:

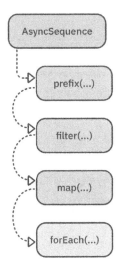

The implementation is so simple that you'll add it directly in **BlabberModel.swift**.

At the bottom of the source file, after any of the existing declarations, add:

```
extension AsyncSequence {
  func forEach(_ body: (Element) async throws -> Void) async
throws {

  }
}
```

In this new extension, you add a method to *all types* that conform to `AsyncSequence`, which takes an asynchronous, throwing closure and returns no result.

Next, add the implementation inside the new method:

```
for try await element in self {
  try await body(element)
}
```

You asynchronously iterate over the sequence values and, as soon as any of them is available, pass it to `body(_:)`.

Now, you have your own extension to *all* asynchronous sequences. If sometimes you feel like `for await` is too wordy, you can use `forEach` instead.

To try the new method, scroll to countdown(to:) and replace the for await loop with:

```
try await counter.forEach { [weak self] in
  try await self?.say($0)
}
```

Arguably, the code isn't much less wordy than the for await loop, because BlabberModel is a class — so you need to add all the cruft to avoid retain cycles by weakly capturing self.

However, in use cases where you're working with a struct instead of a class, you'd be able to use it simply as: try await counter.forEach(say).

It's time to congratulate yourself! With that last addition to the project code, you've finished working through this chapter. AsyncStream is one of the most powerful tools in your async/await toolbox.

If you had fun bridging existing APIs like Timer and NotificationCenter, you'll *love* the next chapter, where you'll learn how to bridge *any code* with the special **continuation** APIs. Before you move on, however, you can learn more about AsyncStream by completing this chapter's optional challenge.

# Challenges

## Challenge: Using AsyncStream(unfolding:onCancel:)

In the `AsyncStream` overview section, you read about two ways to initialize an asynchronous stream. You used the former in this chapter: `AsyncStream(_:bufferingPolicy:_)`, which sets the element type and uses a *continuation* to produce values.

The latter — `AsyncStream(unfolding:onCancel:)` — is a little simpler to use. Its closure parameter does *not* use a continuation. Instead, it returns either values or `nil` to terminate the sequence. Put simply, the `unfolding` closure is your iterator's `next()` method.

For this challenge, go back and revisit the `counter` sequence in `BlabberModel.countdown(to:)`.

Rewrite the code to use `AsyncStream(unfolding:onCancel:)` instead of `AsyncStream(_:bufferingPolicy:_)`. For this exercise, omit the `onCancel` parameter.

Remember that returning `nil` from the `unfolding` closure terminates the sequence.

When implementing the `unfolding` closure, follow the code structure below:

1. Use `Task.sleep` to sleep a billion nanoseconds: `1_000_000_000`. If `Task.sleep` throws, it means the current task is canceled and you can safely finish the sequence.

2. Use `defer` to decrease your counter when the closure execution completes.

3. Return "N …" when the counter is greater than zero.

4. Return "🦊 message" if the counter has reached zero.

5. Otherwise — complete the sequence.

The completed sequence workflow should like this:

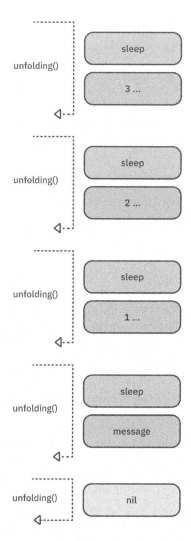

As always, if you get stuck or want to compare your code, look at the **challenges** project for this chapter.

# Key points

- You can use **iterators** and **loops** to implement your own processing logic when consuming an AsyncSequence.

- AsyncSequence and its partner in crime, AsyncIteratorProtocol, let you easily create your own asynchronous sequences.

- AsyncStream is the easiest way to create asynchronous sequences from a single Swift closure.

- When working with a continuation: Use yield(_:) to produce a value, yield(with:) to both produce a value and finish the sequence or finish() to indicate the sequence completed.

# Chapter 5: Intermediate async/await & CheckedContinuation

By Marin Todorov

In the previous chapter, you worked through creating custom asynchronous sequences. At this point, you should already feel right at home when it comes to using `AsyncSequence` and `AsyncStream`.

You saw that wrapping existing APIs, like `Timer` and `NotificationCenter`, is very powerful, letting you reuse your tried-and-tested code in your modern `async/await` codebase.

In this chapter, you'll continue working in the same direction. You'll look into more ways to reuse existing code to the fullest by leveraging Swift's superpowered concurrency features.

# Introducing continuations

Two patterns form the cornerstone of asynchronous programming on Apple platforms: callbacks and the delegate pattern. With completion callbacks, you pass in a closure that executes when the work completes. With the delegate pattern, you create a delegate object, then call certain methods on it when work progresses or completes:

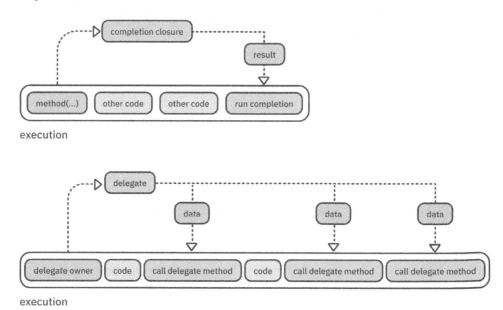

To encourage the new concurrency model's adoption, Apple designed a minimal but powerful API that comes in handy when bridging existing code. It centers around the concept of a **continuation**.

A continuation is an object that tracks a program's state at a given point. The Swift concurrency model assigns each asynchronous unit of work a continuation instead of creating an entire thread for it. This allows the concurrency model to scale your work more effectively based on the capabilities of the hardware. It creates only as many threads as there are available CPU cores, and it switches between continuations instead of between threads, making it more efficient.

You're familiar with how an `await` call works: Your current code **suspends** execution and hands the thread and system resources over to the central handler, which decides what to do next.

When the awaited function completes, your original code resumes, as long as no higher priority tasks are pending. But how?

When the original code suspends, it creates a continuation that represents the entire captured state at the point of suspension. When it's time to resume execution or throw, the concurrency system recreates the state from the continuation and the work... well, *continues*.

```
  ┌──────────────────────────────────────────────────────┐
  ┆-▷func hello() async throws -> String {                ┆
  ┆      try await Task.sleep(nanoseconds: 1_000_000)     ┆
  ┆      return "Hello world"┆ resume                      ┆
  ┆  }        ┆··············· ┆                           ┆
  ┆           ▽                            suspend         ┆
  ┆  let result = try await hello()·······················┘
     print(result)
```

This all happens behind the scenes when you use `async` functions. You can also create continuations yourself, which you can use to extend existing code that uses callbacks or delegates. These APIs can benefit from using `await` as well.

Manually creating continuations allows you to migrate your existing code gradually to the new concurrency model.

# Creating continuations manually

There are two continuation API variants:

1. **CheckedContinuation**: A mechanism to resume a suspended execution or throw an error. It provides runtime checks for correct usage and logs any misuse.

2. **UnsafeContinuation**: An alternative to `CheckedContinuation`, but without the safety checks. Use this when performance is essential and you don't need the extra safety.

> **Note**: The APIs are essentially identical, so you'll only work with `CheckedContinuation` in this chapter. For any function mentioned in this chapter that has "checked" in its name, you can assume there's an "unsafe" equivalent as well.

You don't normally initialize a continuation yourself. Instead, you use one of two handy generic functions that take a closure. The closure provides a ready-to-use continuation as an input parameter:

- **withCheckedContinuation(_:)**: Wraps the closure and gives you a checked continuation back.

- **withCheckedThrowingContinuation(_:)**: Wraps a throwing closure. Use this when you need error handling.

You **must** resume the continuation once — and exactly once. Enforcing this rule is the difference between checked and unsafe continuations. You resume a continuation by using one of the following ways:

- **resume()**: Resumes the suspended task without a value.

- **resume(returning:)**: Resumes the suspended task and returns the given value.

- **resume(throwing:)**: Resumes the suspended task, throwing the provided error.

- **resume(with:)**: Resumes with a `Result` containing a value or an error.

The methods above are the only ones you can call on a continuation, which is yet another easy-to-use, minimal type.

Next, you'll wrap `CLLocationManagerDelegate` to learn how to quickly use continuations to reuse your existing code.

## Wrapping the delegate pattern

In this chapter, you'll continue working on the Blabber project, starting where you left off at the end of the last chapter. If you've worked through the challenges, just keep up the great work. Otherwise, you can start with this chapter's starter project, which includes the solved challenge.

Start the book server now, if you haven't already. Navigate to the server folder in the book materials-repository, **00-book-server**, and enter `swift run`. The detailed steps are covered in Chapter 1, "Why Modern Swift Concurrency?".

Some APIs use the delegate pattern to continuously "talk" to their delegate — for example, to send progress updates or notifications about app state changes. When you need to handle multiple values, you should use an `AsyncStream` to bridge the delegate pattern to newer code.

In other cases, like in this chapter, you'll need to handle a single delegation callback or a completion — and that's the perfect opportunity to use a continuation!

In the next few sections, you'll focus on letting the users share their location in chat:

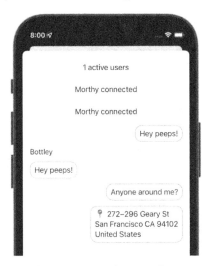

When you work with location data, you need to reach out to one of the oldest frameworks in iOS: `CoreLocation`.

> **Note**: Offering apps that were capable of providing location-based services was one of the iPhone 2's killer features — and one of the reasons why it became a huge success. `CoreLocation` is one of the frameworks that iOS 2 initially made available to third-party developers.

As a *classic* API, `CoreLocation` heavily relies on delegates, making it a perfect candidate for you to learn how to interoperate between `async/await` code and those older patterns.

The main type you usually deal with in the CoreLocation framework is CLLocationManager. When you ask this type to start location updates, it repeatedly calls its delegate with the current device location:

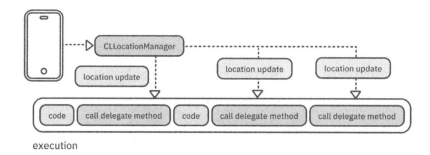

In Blabber, you don't want to share the user location continuously, but only once — when the user taps the location button. Still, the location manager doesn't provide a callback API that lets you get just a single location. You'll need to create your own delegate type and code the logic to stop updates after the first location comes through.

Open **BlabberModel.swift** and scroll to shareLocation(). This method is already wired to the location button in the chat screen:

# Managing the authorizations

You'll get started by creating a location manager and verifying that the user has authorized the app to use the device location data. At this point, users who are running the app for the first time will see the standard system dialogue that asks them to grant authorization:

Before dealing with any `CoreLocation`-specific work, add the following code that creates a continuation:

```
let location: CLLocation = try await
  withCheckedThrowingContinuation { [weak self] continuation in

}
```

`withCheckedThrowingContinuation(_:)` takes a throwing closure, suspends the current task, then executes the closure. You should call your asynchronous code from within the closure, then resume the `continuation` argument when you're done. In this case, you'll resume with an error or a location.

You can pass `continuation` around like any other variable, storing it in your model or passing it over to other functions. Wherever it ends up, calling one of its `resume(...)` methods will always resume the execution at the original call site.

Also, you might have noticed that the function contains "checked" in its name. That indicates the **runtime** checks if you use the continuation safely.

Build and run the project. Tap the location button, and then tap **Allow While Using App** in the privacy dialogue:

Log in and tap the location button. You won't see an error onscreen. However, look at the Xcode console output, and you'll see the following, between other logs:

```
SWIFT TASK CONTINUATION MISUSE: shareLocation() leaked its
continuation!
```

The runtime detected that you never used `continuation` and that the variable was released at the end of the closure. Long story short, your code at `try await withCheckedThrowingContinuation(...)` will never successfully resume from its suspension point.

As mentioned earlier, you *must* call a `resume(...)` method exactly once from each code path.

Next, you'll fix this by integrating your `continuation` with a newly minted delegate.

## Handling the location errors

Open **Utility/ChatLocationDelegate.swift**, where you'll find the placeholder type `ChatLocationDelegate`. Notice that all the `CLLocationManagerDelegate` requirements are optional, so the file compiles without any of `CLLocationManagerDelegate`'s methods.

You'll add two methods to handle location updates and location errors.

First of all, inside the class definition, add a new type alias for a throwing continuation that returns a location:

```
typealias LocationContinuation = CheckedContinuation<CLLocation,
Error>
```

That alias name will make your code a little less verbose.

Since your delegate holds on to the continuation until it receives a location, you need to store it in a property. You'll also add a `CLLocationManager` to feed your proxy delegate with any updates. Add both of these properties, like so:

```
private var continuation: LocationContinuation?
private let manager = CLLocationManager()
```

You also need a new initializer so you can **inject** the continuation and also ask the location manager for the needed permissions. Add that next:

```
init(continuation: LocationContinuation) {
  self.continuation = continuation
  super.init()
  manager.delegate = self
  manager.requestWhenInUseAuthorization()
}
```

First of all, note the use of super.init(); this lets you set self as the location manager's delegate *before* requesting authorization.

Then, you call requestWhenInUseAuthorization() to show the system privacy dialogue, which sets the authorization status on the manager object. If the user has already granted permissions, the method does nothing. You'll deal with the various authorization values later in the chapter.

> **Note**: You'll need to grant location permissions to continue with this chapter. If you denied location usage by mistake, or you wanted to test what happens if you rejected the permissions, don't worry — just delete the app from the iOS Simulator. The next time you run the project, you'll get the authorization dialogue again.

The first delegate method you need is the one that gets called when the location permissions update. This happens when the permissions have been granted and immediately after the location manager is created. Add the following delegate method to ChatLocationDelegate:

```
func locationManagerDidChangeAuthorization(_ manager:
CLLocationManager) {
  switch manager.authorizationStatus {
  case .notDetermined:
    break
  case .authorizedAlways, .authorizedWhenInUse:
    manager.startUpdatingLocation()
  default:
    continuation?.resume(
      throwing: "The app isn't authorized to use location data"
    )
    continuation = nil
  }
}
```

If the user hasn't responded to the permissions request, which would happen the first time they run the app, you do nothing. If they've granted the permissions, you tell the location manager to start getting location data. Otherwise, you'll resume the continuation with an error.

After resuming, you destroy the continuation because doing anything else with it is illegal.

Next, add the delegate method that's called when the user's location updates:

```
func locationManager(
  _ manager: CLLocationManager,
  didUpdateLocations locations: [CLLocation]
) {
  guard let location = locations.first else { return }
  continuation?.resume(returning: location)
  continuation = nil
}
```

The `locations` argument contains a list of `CLLocation` values. Here, it's safe to take the first one and pass it on to your own code.

Additionally, you call `continuation?.resume(returning:)` to resume the original code execution and return the first location from the suspension point:

```
                                                          resume
  let location: CLLocation = try await withCheckedThrowingContinuation { continuation
  ...........................................................................

    func locationManager(_ manager: CLLocationManager,
      didUpdateLocations locations: [CLLocation]) {

      guard let location = locations.first else { return }
      continuation?.resume(returning: location)
      continuation = nil
    }
```

Finally, just like before, you set the `continuation` property to `nil`.

Next, add error handling via `locationManager(_:didFailWithError:)`:

```
func locationManager(
  _ manager: CLLocationManager,
  didFailWithError error: Error
) {
  continuation?.resume(throwing: error)
  continuation = nil
}
```

If the manager fails to fetch the device location, it calls this method on its delegate so you can update your app accordingly.

You use `continuation?.resume(throwing:)` to resume your original code at the suspension point and throw the given error:

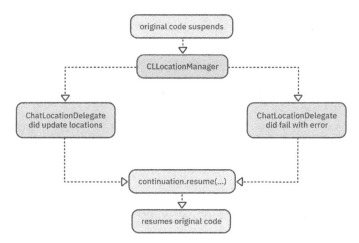

At the end, as you did before, you set `continuation` to `nil` to release the continuation you just used.

You now have the complete workflow in place: Once you set up the location manager with the delegate, it will try to fetch the current location and will call one of the methods you've wired to use the injected `continuation`:

Additionally, when the continuation resumes, you reset `continuation` so you can't use it more than once.

This concludes the setup. Now, it's time to start the updates and set the whole machinery in motion.

# Using your delegate

Inside the closure of `withCheckedThrowingContinuation(_:)`, insert the following:

```
self?.delegate = ChatLocationDelegate(continuation:
continuation)
```

You just created a `ChatLocationDelegate` and injected the `continuation` you got
from `withCheckedThrowingContinuation(_:)` to it. You store the resulting
delegate to a predefined `delegate` property to make sure it isn't immediately
released from memory.

After that, what happens is:

1.  The manager calls the change authorization delegate method when it initializes.

2.  After the user grants permissions, the manager fetches the device location.

3.  The manager calls the delegate with an array of `CLLocations`.

4.  The delegate calls `continuation` and resumes by returning the first available
    `CLLocation`.

5.  The original call site `let location: CLLocation = try await`
    `withCheckedThrowingContinuation ...` resumes execution, letting you use
    the returned location value.

To test the result, append the following code at the very bottom of the function, after
`withCheckedThrowingContinuation`:

```
print(location.description)
```

When the process completes, you'll see the location object printed in Xcode's
console.

Build and run. Tap the location button to give the new feature a try.

There could be two outcomes of this. You will either see a location printed in the output console if you've used Xcode to simulate location data in the past. Alternatively, you will see an error like so:

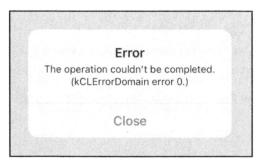

By the way — how *cool* is that?

You didn't write any special code to handle the error — you pipe in the error from your delegate, then your continuation re-throws it. Finally, you catch the error seamlessly in the button action. For the last mile, the starter SwiftUI code updates lastErrorMessage on the chat view, which pops the alert box onscreen.

If you haven't tested location-aware apps in Xcode before, you need to enable location data in the iOS Simulator.

At the bottom of the code editor in Xcode, click the location button and pick one of the default locations in the list:

Once you're feeding location data successfully into the iOS Simulator, you'll see the location icon fill with color:

Log in again and tap the location button. This time, you'll see the coordinates of your selected location in the console:

```
<+19.01761470,+72.85616440> +/- 5.00m (speed -1.00 mps / course
-1.00) ...
```

Great work so far! You've gone through setting up a continuation and creating a proxy delegate. Now, you can apply this approach in basically any scenario.

To exercise this routine one more time, you'll look into wrapping up a callback-based API next.

# Wrapping callback APIs with continuation

In the system frameworks that Apple introduced after iOS 4, most asynchronous APIs are callback-based.

That means that when you call a given method, you provide a parameter with a closure that executes asynchronously when the method finishes its work.

For example, if your app wants to request authorization to provide parental controls, you need to call
`AuthorizationCenter.requestAuthorization(completionHandler:)` from Apple's **FamilyControls** framework, like so:

```
AuthorizationCenter.shared
  .requestAuthorization { result in

  }
```

Calling this API displays the system UI that asks for authorization, if necessary. After an arbitrary amount of time, depending on the user's actions, it calls back to your closure. It returns the authorization status via the `result` closure argument.

Having a single closure is arguably a little easier to wrap with a continuation than creating a separate delegate type, as you did earlier in the chapter.

In this section, you'll continue working on BlabberModel.shareLocation() by wrapping a custom callback-based API that turns a location into a human-readable address.

The Blabber starter project includes a custom type called AddressEncoder. It converts a location to a human-readable address via a classic callback API: AddressEncoder.addressFor(location:completion:).

In this section, you'll work through calling that API and using a continuation to make it fit seamlessly with the rest of your asynchronous code.

## Creating the closure

Open **BlabberModel.swift** and scroll back to the method called shareLocation(), where you added your delegate wrapping code.

To make the new call to AddressEncoder, add this code at the bottom of shareLocation():

```
let address: String = try await
  withCheckedThrowingContinuation { continuation in

}
```

You start this section the same way that you approached wrapping CLLocationManager's delegate — by calling withCheckedThrowingContinuation(_:) to create a closure with a continuation to control asynchronous execution.

This time, you'll return a String when you resume. That string will be the human-friendly address for the location coordinates you already have.

Now, insert this code inside the closure:

```
AddressEncoder.addressFor(location: location) { address, error
  in

}
```

Here, you call addressFor(location:completion:). In the completion callback, you receive an optional address and an optional error.

This is, unfortunately, a common pattern in Swift APIs, especially before the official introduction of the Result type.

This pattern opens the code for undesired scenarios — for example, when the closure receives both a `nil` result and a `nil` error...

You'll have to make the best of the situation and try resuming with the correct behavior for each callback outcome. Add this `switch` inside the callback closure from above:

```
switch (address, error) {
case (nil, let error?):
  continuation.resume(throwing: error)
case (let address?, nil):
  continuation.resume(returning: address)
}
```

You switch over `address` and `error`:

- When you get an error, you pipe it through to the continuation via `continuation.resume(throwing:)`.

- On the other hand, if you get an address back, you return it via `continuation.resume(returning:)`.

So far, so good — but the compiler now complains that you need to handle *all* the possible combinations.

Add two more cases inside the `switch` statement to handle any unexpected callback input:

```
case (nil, nil):
  continuation.resume(throwing: "Address encoding failed")
case let (address?, error?):
  continuation.resume(returning: address)
  print(error)
}
```

- If you get `nil` for both the address and the error, that's clearly some kind of unknown error, so you throw a generic error: **Address encoding failed**.

- If you get both an address *and* an error, you return the address — but also print the error so that the message remains in the app's log.

That clears the compiler error, and you cover all the bases when it comes to unexpected callbacks from `AddressEncoder`.

> **Note**: If you already peeked into the source code of `AddressEncoder`, you know that it will never call the completion closure with incorrect parameters. However, you can't do that for APIs where you don't have access to the source code. That's why it's important to handle invalid API usage defensively.

It's time for the final line in `shareLocation()`. After your new `withCheckedThrowingContinuation`, append:

```
try await say(" 📍 \(address)")
```

Once you have the address as a string, you call `BlabberModel.say(_:)` to share it in chat.

Build and run one more time. Enable location simulation in Xcode and tap the location button in the app:

With that last addition to the Blabber app, you've covered most of the continuation APIs, and you've used continuations to bridge delegates and callbacks. Doing this will allow your `async/await` code to work *alongside* your existing codebase, not *against* it.

You'll continue working with Blabber in the next chapter, where you'll learn more about debugging and testing your asynchronous code.

If you'd like to work through one more exercise, stay around for this chapter's optional challenge.

# Challenges

## Challenge: Build a command-line version of Blabber

This is an *optional* challenge that you can try on your own to exercise some of the concepts of the last few chapters.

In this challenge, you'll build the Clipper app: a CLI (Command Line Interface) version of Blabber. It lets you grab a user name and chat with friends from a Terminal window.

In the introduction section of Chapter 1, "Why Modern Swift Concurrency?", you covered platform restrictions for Swift concurrency features. As a reminder, you're building a macOS app here. That means that if you're using Xcode 13.2 or newer, you can run this challenge on macOS 10.15 or later. If you're using an earlier version of Xcode 13, you have to be running macOS 12.

This project's twist is that, as a command-line app, it's an exercise in creating a complete chat app in about 30 lines of code.

When you've successfully completed the challenge, you'll be able to open multiple Terminal windows and chat between your alter egos.

Open the starter challenge project for this chapter by double-clicking **Package.swift**. The Clipper app consists of a single source file called **main.swift**.

Inside, you'll find:

- A long-living `URLSession` for live updates called `liveURLSession`.

- One `Task` that accesses the `/cli/chat` server endpoint. Its job is to print the chat messages.

- A second `Task` that iterates over the standard user input and sends any messages the user enters to the server.

Believe it or not — that's the complete chat app!

You can try completing the code on your own; if you prefer the guided tour, however, follow these steps:

1.  Inside the do block in the first `Task`, get a `bytes` stream of the `url` address defined in the task. Then, iterate over the lines, like you did in previous chapters, and print each line. Use `liveURLSession` so the request doesn't time out.

That's all! To test the chat, follow these steps:

- Start the book server.

- Open multiple Terminal windows.

- In each window, change the current directory to the Clipper folder — the folder containing **Package.swift**.

- In each window, type `swift run Clipper [username]` and replace [username] with the chat name you'd like to use.

- You'll see a message from the server confirming you're connected: `[username connected]`.

- Now, you can chat by entering messages in each Terminal.

# Key points

- You bridge older asynchronous design patterns to `async`/`await` by using `CheckedContinuation` or its unsafe counterpart, `UnsafeCheckedContinuation`.

- For each of your code paths, you need to call one of the continuation's `resume(...)` methods **exactly once** to either return a value or throw an error.

- You get a continuation by calling either `withCheckedContinuation(_:)` or `withCheckedThrowingContinuation(_:)`.

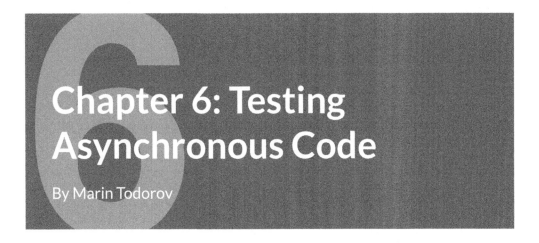

# Chapter 6: Testing Asynchronous Code

By Marin Todorov

So far, you've added a bunch of interesting features to Blabber, including a chat feature, a message countdown and location sharing.

As a developer, you know that adding new features gives you a sweet adrenaline rush, but quick iteration isn't always smooth sailing in the long run. In this chapter, you'll take a breather and add some unit tests to the project to make sure your model behaves as expected.

Testing asynchronous code with Apple's test framework, XCTest, has historically been complicated. Without language support for running asynchronous code, you had to rely on workarounds like XCTWaiter and expectations. Additionally, you had to wait until the test under code was complete before you could verify its output.

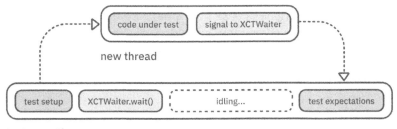

From what you've learned so far in this book, you might think you need to do something complicated to make an asynchronous context within your testing code. Luckily, you don't! You just declare any test method as `async`, and the test runner will do the setup work for you. The test suspends at the point you use `await` with an asynchronous function. Once it resumes, you can verify the output as usual:

test execution

As you see in the diagram above, the new syntax lets you write asynchronous tests linearly, *as if* they were synchronous. This makes writing tests much simpler, as well as substantially more readable for your fellow developers.

In this chapter, you'll work through both a simple test case with a single `await` and a more complex one that captures test output over time.

# Capturing network calls under test

Open the starter version of Blabber in this chapter's materials, under **projects/ starter**. Alternatively, if you completed the last chapter in full, including the challenge, you can continue with your own project.

Next, open **BlabberTests.swift**, where you'll add your tests for the `BlabberModel` type. So far, there are no tests. No bueno!

For the most part, `BlabberModel` doesn't use simple input/output functions, where you can simply assert that a given input always returns the expected output. Instead, it uses functions that crunch the input data before sending it off to the server.

The full chain of events looks like this:

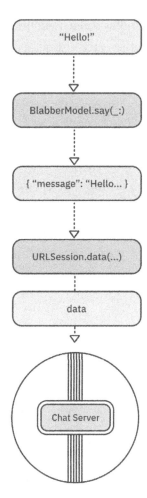

Your goal now is to add asynchronous tests to verify that `BlabberModel` always sends correct data to the server.

Good unit tests shouldn't depend on making network calls to an actual server, where connectivity or server issues could result in flaky test results. There are two common approaches to testing networking calls:

- Injecting a **mock URLSession-like type** that captures requests on your tests' behalf.

- Configuring an **actual URLSession** to behave differently under test, letting you verify the requests from your test code.

In this chapter, you'll work through the second option. Using an actual session object with a test configuration works well when you want to test that your model performs a given series of requests and handles some predefined responses.

You'll add custom URL handlers to your networking stack via `URLSession.configuration`, which lets you do some nifty things. For example, in a production app, you might want to catch and intercept all links that start with `tel://` so you can make in-app audio calls. Or you might custom-handle URLs starting with `https://youtube.com` to prevent your users from switching to the YouTube app.

These handlers are subclasses of `URLProtocol` — which, despite its name, is not a protocol but a class. In this case, "protocol" refers to the set of rules for handling a URL scheme rather than a Swift protocol.

For your tests in this chapter, you'll intercept and record *all* network requests using a custom `URLProtocol` subclass:

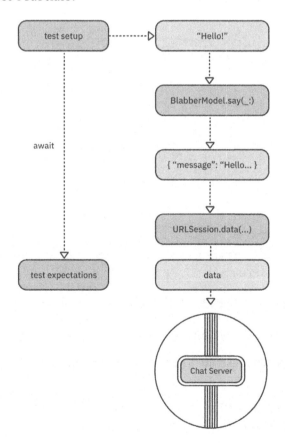

# Implementing a custom URLProtocol

Open **Utility/TestURLProtocol.swift**. Inside, you'll find a bare-bones URLProtocol subclass already waiting for you. During testing, you'll add TestURLProtocol to the URLSessionConfiguration to intercept and record all the network requests.

The minimum protocol requirements, which are already included in the code, are:

- **canInit(with:)**: Returns true when the current protocol should handle the given URLRequest. In this case, you always return true since you want to catch *all* requests.

- **canonicalRequest(for:)**: This method can alter requests on the fly. In this case, you simply return the given request with no changes.

- **startLoading()**: Here, you load the request and send a response back to the client.

- **stopLoading()**: Call this method when the operation is canceled or when the session should otherwise stop the request. For these tests, you don't have to add anything here.

The starter code in startLoading() creates a successful server response with no content and returns it to the client. For these tests, you're only interested in the outgoing requests, not what comes back from the server. You'll also record the network requests here.

Next, add this new property to the TestURLProtocol type:

```
static var lastRequest: URLRequest?
```

Each time TestURLProtocol responds to a request, you'll store it in lastRequest so you can verify its contents.

You probably noticed that the property is static. Because of the way you pass these URL protocols to URLSessionConfiguration, you can't easily access instance properties, as you'll see in a moment. For the simple tests in this chapter, this will do just fine.

Next, add the code to store each request at the bottom of startLoading():

```
guard let stream = request.httpBodyStream else {
  fatalError("Unexpected test scenario")
}

var request = request
request.httpBody = stream.data
self.lastRequest = request
```

In this block, you take several steps:

- First, you verify that the request has a non-nil httpBodyStream input stream. That's the stream you use to read the request data.

- You make a new mutable request variable so you can modify the request before storing it.

- You read the request contents from httpBodyStream and store the data in httpBody.

- Finally, you save the request in lastRequest so your tests can verify the contents after the network call completes.

That's all it takes to complete your custom catch-all URL protocol. Now, you just need to use it to spy on what your app is sending.

## Creating a model for testing

Switch back to **BlabberTests.swift** and add a new property in BlabberTests:

```
let model: BlabberModel = {
  // 1
  let model = BlabberModel()
  model.username = "test"

  // 2
  let testConfiguration = URLSessionConfiguration.default
  testConfiguration.protocolClasses = [TestURLProtocol.self]

  // 3
  model.urlSession = URLSession(configuration:
testConfiguration)
  return model
}()
```

Here's what the code above does:

1.  Create a new `BlabberModel` with the given username.

2.  Create a URL session configuration that uses `TestURLProtocol` to handle URL requests.

3.  Tell the model to use this new session.

`TestURLProtocol` will handle all the network calls made by this instance of `BlabberModel` so you can inspect them in your tests.

Now, it's time to write a test!

# Adding a simple asynchronous test

A critical point to remember when adding asynchronous tests is to add the `async` keyword to each test method. Doing this lets you `await` your code under test and easily verify the output.

Add the following method to `BlabberTests` to create your first test:

```
func testModelSay() async throws {
  try await model.say("Hello!")

}
```

Since the model is already configured to use the test-suitable URL session, you don't need to do any additional setup — you just call `say(_:)` right away.

At this point, you're ready to add your test expectations. First, you'll verify that the last request the network performed, `model.say("Hello!")`, was sent to the correct URL.

Add the following code to do that:

```
let request = try XCTUnwrap(TestURLProtocol.lastRequest)

XCTAssertEqual(
  request.url?.absoluteString,
  "http://localhost:8080/chat/say"
)
```

You first unwrap the optional `TestURLProtocol.lastRequest`, then check that the URL matches the expected address: `http://localhost:8080/chat/say`.

Now that you've verified that the model sends the data to the correct endpoint, you can check that it also sends the correct data.

Finish up your test with the following piece of code:

```
let httpBody = try XCTUnwrap(request.httpBody)
let message = try XCTUnwrap(try? JSONDecoder()
  .decode(Message.self, from: httpBody))

XCTAssertEqual(message.message, "Hello!")
```

You expect `request.httpBody` to decode as a `Message`. Once decoded, you assert that the message text equals **"Hello!"**, as expected.

If you wrote asynchronous tests prior to Swift 5.5, you're likely excited about the brevity and clarity of this test code. And if you haven't written asynchronous tests before, you really don't need to know the lengths you had to go to set up a good asynchronous test back then!

To run the test, click **Play** in the editor gutter, to the left of `func testModelSay()`..., or press **Command-U** to run all tests.

Regardless of how you go about it, you'll see the test **pass** and a green check mark (the best check mark!) will appear next to the test name in Xcode:

```
46
       func testModelSay() async throws {
48        try await model.say("Hello!")
49
50        let request = try XCTUnwrap(TestURLProtocol.lastRequest)
51
```

# Testing values over time with AsyncStream

Now that you've created a test that awaits a single value, you'll move on to testing asynchronous work that may yield *many* values.

Start by adding another test to **BlabberTests.swift**:

```
func testModelCountdown() async throws {

}
```

As you already guessed, this test verifies if `BlabberModel.countdown(to:)` behaves as expected.

This time around, you're in for a much more complex testing scenario, so be prepared to brace!

> **Note**: Some tests are simply more challenging to design than others. If a given piece of code is difficult to test, that usually means you can improve the code itself — for example, by breaking it down into logical pieces and making it more composable. But sometimes, depending on the situation, tests are just complex. However, you'll see that using `async/await` makes even complex tests easier to design.

Your `say(_:)` test was fairly simple because the method does a single thing and only sends a single network request:

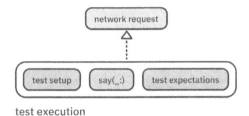

`countdown(to:)`, in comparison, is more involved. It sends up to four network requests, so you can't verify only the last one in the sequence to guarantee the method works correctly:

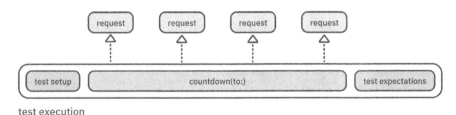

This is really *nice* for you because it gives you the opportunity to use some of the new modern concurrency APIs.

Switch back to **TestURLProtocol.swift**. There, you store the last accepted request in `lastRequest`. Now, you'll add a new function that returns a **stream of all requests**. You'll then be able to call `countdown(to:)` and verify all the requests it sent.

To start, add the following code to `TestURLProtocol`:

```
static private var continuation:
AsyncStream<URLRequest>.Continuation?

static var requests: AsyncStream<URLRequest> = {
  return AsyncStream { continuation in
    TestURLProtocol.continuation = continuation
  }
}()
```

This code adds a static property holding a continuation as well as a new static property, `requests`, which returns an asynchronous stream that emits requests.

You call `finish()` on the first line, just in case there's an old continuation from a previous test. Then, you create a new `AsyncStream` and store its continuation.

You need to store the continuation so you can emit a value each time `TestURLProtocol` responds to a request. This is easy to handle — you just add a `didSet` handler to `lastRequest`.

Replace the `lastRequest` property declaration with this code:

```
static var lastRequest: URLRequest? {
  didSet {
    if let request = lastRequest {
      continuation?.yield(request)
    }
  }
}
```

Now, updating `lastRequest` will also emit the request as an element of the asynchronous stream that `requests` returns.

Great, these are all the changes you need to make in `TestURLProtocol`!

## Completing the countdown test

Switch back to **BlabberTests.swift** and scroll to `testModelCountdown()`. It's time to finally add your test code.

Add this code to `testModelCountdown()`:

```
try await model.countdown(to: "Tada!")
for await request in TestURLProtocol.requests {
  print(request)
}
```

Here's what the code above is doing:

1.  Make a call to `countdown(to:)`.

2.  Iterate over the stream of requests to print the recorded values.

Run the test by clicking **Play** in the editor gutter:

```
     func testModelCountdown() async throws {
69       try await model.countdown(to: "Tada!")
70       for await request in TestURLProtocol.requests {
71         print(request)
72       }
73     }
74   }
```

Let the test run for a while... sadly, the execution never completes. The logs in Xcode's output console prove that the test is hanging:

```
Test Suite 'Selected tests' started at 2021-09-02 13:53:33.107
Test Suite 'BlabberTests.xctest' started at 2021-09-02
13:53:33.108
Test Suite 'BlabberTests' started at 2021-09-02 13:53:33.109
Test Case '-[BlabberTests.BlabberTests testModelCountdown]'
started.
```

As per the last log message, the test runner started `testModelCountdown`, but it never completed.

Next, add breakpoints on all three of the lines you just added and run the test again to verify where the execution stops:

```
     func testModelCountdown() async throws {
69       try await model.countdown(to: "Tada!")
70       for await request in TestURLProtocol.requests {
71         print(request)
72       }
73     }
74   }
```

The debugger stops on the first and second lines, but it never hits the breakpoint on `print(request)`. The stream never emits any values.

What's going on here? Look back at how you emit the requests: You only emit values when `lastRequest` is set. When your test starts the `for await` loop, `countdown(to:)` has already finished, so there are no requests to read.

It seems like you'll have to scrap the current code and take a new approach. There's one *essential* thing you should notice during this exercise:

`await` **does not time out**!

That means that if some of the tested code doesn't behave correctly, your tests will just **hang forever** at some `await` suspension point.

This is not a problem with your test, *per se*. `await` simply doesn't time out at all. If that turns into a problem in your code, you can fix this by adding some custom code to cancel your task if it takes longer than expected to complete.

You'll take a quick detour from finishing `testModelCountdown()` and do just that — add the supporting infrastructure to your tests so they safely time out, instead of hanging forever.

# Adding TimeoutTask for safer testing

You can't let your tests hang indefinitely — that would defeat the purpose of verifying incorrect behavior. Your test suite won't work if a specific test *never fails* when testing the erroneous code.

In this section, you'll create a new type called `TimeoutTask`. This type is similar to `Task` except that it will throw an error if the asynchronous code doesn't complete in time.

In the **Utility** folder inside **BlabberTests**, create a new file called **TimeoutTask.swift**.

Since you'll use that file in your tests, take a moment after creating it to double-check that it only belongs to your test target. You can verify this under the **Target Membership** section in the File inspector on the right-hand side of the Xcode window while you have **TimeoutTask.swift** open:

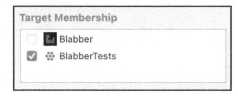

If you haven't checked the checkbox next to **BlabberTests**, do so now.

Next, replace *all* of the code in your new file with:

```
import Foundation

class TimeoutTask<Success> {

}

extension TimeoutTask {
  struct TimeoutError: LocalizedError {
    var errorDescription: String? {
      return "The operation timed out."
    }
  }
}
```

Here, you create a new type that is generic over Success, just like Swift's Task is. Success is the type of result the task returns, if any. If the task doesn't return a result, then Success is Void.

Additionally, you define a TimeoutError, which you'll throw if the task times out.

With the basic setup out of the way, you can add the initializer for TimeoutTask, too, along with some useful properties:

```
let nanoseconds: UInt64
let operation: @Sendable () async throws -> Success

init(
  seconds: TimeInterval,
  operation: @escaping @Sendable () async throws -> Success
) {
  self.nanoseconds = UInt64(seconds * 1_000_000_000)
  self.operation = operation
}
```

The first parameter of your new initializer is the maximum duration in seconds, which you convert to nanoseconds and store. The second parameter is operation, which is (deep breath...) an escaping, thread-safe, asynchronous, throwing closure.

To go through all of those keywords:

- **@escaping**: Indicates that you may store and execute the closure outside of the initializer's scope.

- **@Sendable**: You can't conform to protocols for closures or function types in the same way that you can with other types. This new keyword indicates that a closure or function type conforms to the Sendable protocol, meaning it's safe to transfer between concurrency domains.

- **async**: Hopefully, you're familiar with this term by now. It means the closure should execute in a concurrent asynchronous context.

- **throws**: The closure can throw an error.

That's a cumbersome set of keywords, but they all help the compiler and the runtime clearly understand your intentions and run your code correctly.

The initializer doesn't do anything other than storing its values. Here, it differs from Task, which starts executing immediately.

> **Note**: You'll learn more about the Sendable protocol and the @Sendable annotation for function parameters in Chapter 8, "Getting Started With Actors".

## Starting the task and returning its result

Next, you'll add a property called value, which will start the work and asynchronously return the result of the task. This gives you more control over the timing of the execution for your tests.

Add the following code to TimeoutTask:

```
private var continuation: CheckedContinuation<Success, Error>?

var value: Success {
  get async throws {
    try await withCheckedThrowingContinuation { continuation in
      self.continuation = continuation
    }
  }
}
```

As you've done in previous chapters, you declare the value getter as async and throws so you can control execution asynchronously.

Inside the getter, you start by calling withCheckedThrowingContinuation(_:) to get a continuation. This lets you either complete successfully or throw an error if the operation times out.

Once you get the initialized continuation, you store it in the instance property called continuation.

To start implementing the execution logic, add this task immediately after storing the continuation, while still in withCheckedThrowingContinuation's closure:

```
Task {
    try await Task.sleep(nanoseconds: nanoseconds)
    self.continuation?.resume(throwing: TimeoutError())
    self.continuation = nil
}
```

Here, you start an asynchronous task that sleeps for the given number of nanoseconds — the timeout duration you use when creating a TimeoutTask. You then use the stored continuation to throw a TimeoutError().

So far, so good — you've implemented the part of the code that times out. Now, immediately after the previous Task, add the code that does the actual work:

```
Task {
    let result = try await operation()
    self.continuation?.resume(returning: result)
    self.continuation = nil
}
```

In this asynchronous task, you execute the initial operation closure. If that completes successfully, you use continuation to return the result.

You start two asynchronous tasks in parallel and let them race towards the final. Whichever task completes first gets to use the `continuation`, while the slower task gets canceled.

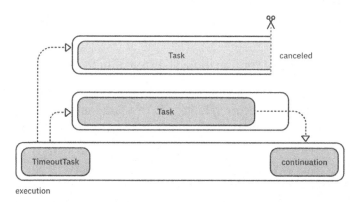

> **Note**: On a rare occasion, it's possible that both tasks might try to use `continuation` at *precisely* the same time — leading to a crash. You'll learn about Swift's `actor` type and writing safe concurrent code in later chapters. For now, leave the `TimeoutTask` code as-is.

## Canceling your task

To wrap up your new type, you'll add one more method: `cancel()`. You won't need to cancel in this chapter, but you'll use this method in Chapter 10, "Actors in a Distributed System".

Inside `TimeoutTask`, add:

```
func cancel() {
  continuation?.resume(throwing: CancellationError())
  continuation = nil
}
```

The new method uses the stored `continuation` and throws a `CancellationError()`, like Apple's own asynchronous APIs do when they're canceled.

To try your new task, switch back to **BlabberTests.swift** and wrap the `for await` loop inside `testModelCountdown()` in a `TimeoutTask`, so it looks like this:

```
try await TimeoutTask(seconds: 10) {
  for await request in TestURLProtocol.requests {
    print(request)
  }
}
.value
```

As before, you call `countdown(to:)` and then iterate over `requests` — but this time, you wrap the latter inside a `TimeoutTask` with a maximum duration of ten seconds. You'll also notice you're actually awaiting the task's `value` property, which holds all of the timeout logic you just worked on.

If you still have breakpoints on the test suite, turn them off. Then, run `testModelCountdown()` one more time. After a while, you'll see the test fail:

```
67
     func testModelCountdown() async throws {        ◇ caught error: "The operation timed out."
69     try await model.countdown(to: "Tada!")
70     try await TimeoutTask(seconds: 10) {
71       for await request in TestURLProtocol.requests {
72         print(request)
73       }
74     }
75     .value
76   }
77 }
```

Congratulations, you now have your own `Task` alternative that allows you to write safer asynchronous tests!

Sadly, this indisputable victory does not resolve your initial problem. Even though the test doesn't hang anymore, it still fails. And, to finally be able to ship your progress into your (hypothetical) code repository, your tests need to pass.

# Using async let to produce effects and observe them at the same time

If you remember, the reason the test hangs is that the operations take place in order, and the countdown finishes before you start reading the stored request stream.

You already learned how to start multiple asynchronous tasks and execute them in parallel in Chapter 2, "Getting Started With async/await." You need to make multiple `async let` promises and await them all. That's what you'll do in this test.

Replace the contents of testModelCountdown() one last time with:

```
async let countdown: Void = model.countdown(to: "Tada!")
```

Since countdown(to:) doesn't return a value, you need to explicitly define the promise type as Void. You'll use countdown in a while to await the countdown method along with the task that will observe the recorded network requests.

Now, for the second promise:

```
async let messages = TestURLProtocol.requests
```

If you think about it, you don't really need all the elements in requests. You only need as many as you expect during a successful run of countdown(to:). That means you need four requests, one for each message sent to the server.

Simply add this as the next line, just like you would for a regular Swift sequence:

```
.prefix(4)
```

Because you expect four requests, you take only four elements in the sequence. To collect these four into an array, add one more function call:

```
.reduce(into: []) { result, request in
  result.append(request)
}
```

reduce(...) runs the given closure for each element in the sequence and adds each request to result. Now, you can process the elements as any plain, old collection.

Now, add the following below:

```
.compactMap(\.httpBody)
.compactMap { data in
  try? JSONDecoder()
    .decode(Message.self, from: data)
    .message
}
```

In this code, you:

- Grab httpBody from each of the requests, if it's available.

- Try to decode the body as a Message.

- Return the message property as the result.

Long story short, you collect all the text messages in the messages array, like so:

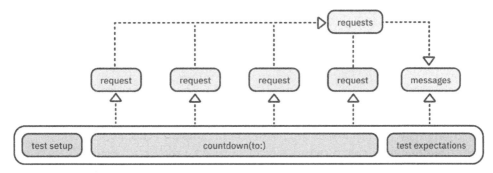

test execution

The code, however, still hangs if you only get three requests instead of the expected four. The execution will stop at prefix(4) and wait for a fourth element.

You need to wrap your messages promise in a TimeoutTask, so messages ends up looking like this:

```
async let messages = TimeoutTask(seconds: 10) {
  await TestURLProtocol.requests
    .prefix(4)
    .reduce(into: []) { result, request in
      result.append(request)
    }
    .compactMap(\.httpBody)
    .compactMap { data in
      try? JSONDecoder()
        .decode(Message.self, from: data).message
    }
}
.value
```

With the two promises ready, the only thing left to do is await them concurrently and verify the output.

Add the following line to await the messages:

```
let (messagesResult, _) = try await (messages, countdown)
```

You don't care about the result of countdown, so you only store messagesResult.

Finally, verify the contents of messagesResult:

```
XCTAssertEqual(
  ["3...", "2...", "1...", "🎉 Tada!"],
  messagesResult
)
```

Run testModelCountdown() once more. This time around, it passes with a green check mark. Fantastic work!

Even though the code is now tested per se, there's one aspect of asynchronous testing that might quickly turn into a problem as your test suite grows. The two unit tests that you just added take over five seconds to complete!

Who has the time to wait for hundreds or thousands of such tests?

# Speeding up asynchronous tests

For both synchronous and asynchronous tests, you often need to inject mock objects that mimic some of your real dependencies, like network calls or accessing a database server.

In this last section of the chapter, you'll inject a "time" dependency in BlabberModel so that time goes a little faster when you're running your tests. Namely, you will use a mock alternative of Task.sleep so that Blabber.countdown(to:) doesn't need to spend so much time waiting.

Open **BlabberModel.swift** and add a new property, where you'll store the sleeping function that the model should use:

```
static var sleep: (UInt64) async throws -> Void =
Task.sleep(nanoseconds:)
```

In the code above, you define a new property called sleep and set its default value to Task.sleep(nanoseconds:). Next, scroll to countdown(to:) and insert the following at the top:

```
let sleep = self.sleep
```

You can use the local copy of the function to do the "sleeping" you'll need a few lines later.

Now, replace the `try await Task.sleep(nanoseconds: 1_000_000_000)` line with:

```
try await sleep(1_000_000_000)
```

Now, your model behaves *exactly the same way* as before by default. But you can easily override the `sleep` property in your tests to change the speed at which the code sleeps.

# Updating the tests

To wrap up, you'll update the tests next. Open **BlabberTests.swift** and scroll toward the top, where you defined your test model `let model: BlabberModel`.

After the line where you inject the test URL session, `model.urlSession`, append this line:

```
model.sleep = { try await Task.sleep(nanoseconds: $0 /
1_000_000_000) }
```

Your test implementation of `sleep` takes the parameter passed to the function, divides it by a billion and calls `Task.sleep(nanoseconds:)` with the result. Effectively, you still implement the same workflow as before and provide the same suspension point at the right moment in the execution. The only difference is that you run the code a billion times faster.

Run the tests one more time by pressing **Command-U** and check the duration. Injecting the test `sleep` function reduces the duration from about 5.5 seconds to around 0.03 seconds on my machine.

Now, you can keep growing your test suite without worrying about how much time it's going to take to run all the tests!

With `async/await` and the modern concurrency APIs, designing asynchronous tests becomes much easier. Nevertheless, the design of your tests depends *mostly* on the code under test. Since your code will vary in nature, you'll always need to create some slightly different setups and conduct tests somewhat differently.

In this chapter, you covered different situations and worked on building your own testing infrastructure. You're now ready to write asynchronous tests in your own apps.

# Key points

- Annotate your test method with `async` to enable testing asynchronous code.

- Use `await` with asynchronous functions to verify their output or side effects after they resume.

- Use either **mock types** for your dependencies or the **real type**, if you can configure it for testing.

- To test time-sensitive asynchronous code, run **concurrent tasks** to both trigger the code under test and observe its output or side effects.

- `await` can suspend indefinitely. So, when testing, it's a good idea to set a **timeout** for the tested asynchronous APIs whenever possible.

# Chapter 7: Concurrent Code With TaskGroup

By Marin Todorov

You've made your way through a lot of new concepts so far. At this point, you're hopefully comfortable with designing code with async/await, creating asynchronous sequences and running tasks in parallel with async let bindings.

async let bindings are a powerful mechanism to help design your asynchronous flow, especially when you have a mix of tasks where some need to run in parallel, while others depend on each other and run sequentially.

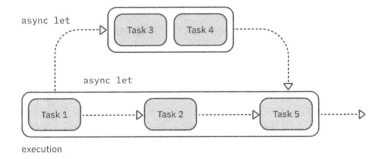

While you have *some* flexibility to decide how many and which tasks to run with async let, that syntax doesn't offer *truly* dynamic concurrency.

Imagine that you need to run a thousand tasks in parallel. Writing async let a thousand times is out of the question! Or what if you don't know in advance how many tasks you need to run in parallel, so you need to write code that can handle that decision at runtime?

Luckily, there's a solution: meet `TaskGroup`, the modern API that allows you to create dynamic concurrency in your code. `TaskGroup` is an elegant API that allows you to create concurrency on the fly, reduces the possibility of data races and lets you safely process the results.

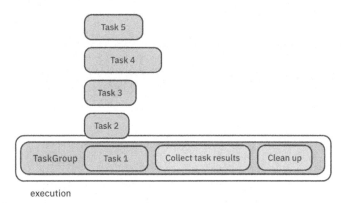

execution

# Introducing TaskGroup

As in previous chapters, you'll start by reading a short overview of the APIs you'll try. You'll then move on to working on a brand new, aliens-related project!

There are two API variants used to construct a task group: `TaskGroup` and `ThrowingTaskGroup`. Like other APIs you've covered in this book, these two variants are almost identical. The difference is that the latter allows for throwing tasks.

You don't initialize a task group yourself — as both APIs don't offer public initializers. Instead, you use one of the following handy generic functions, which creates a group for you and assists the compiler in properly type checking your code:

- **withTaskGroup(of:returning:body:)**: Creates a group with the given task return type, the given return type for the final result you'll construct from tasks in the group, and the body closure as the code that initializes and runs the group.

- **withThrowingTaskGroup(of:returning:body:)**: Takes similar parameters, but each task, as well as the group as a whole, might throw an error.

An important point about these functions is that they *only* return once the group finishes running all of its tasks.

Here's a short example that demonstrates how to use a task group:

```
//1
let images = try await withThrowingTaskGroup(
  of: Data.self
  returning: [UIImage].self
) { group in
  // 2
  for index in 0..<numberOfImages {
    let url = baseURL.appendingPathComponent("image\
(index).png")
    // 3
    group.addTask {
      // 4
      return try await URLSession.shared
        .data(from: url, delegate: nil)
        .0
    }
  }
  // 5
  return try await group.reduce(into: [UIImage]()) { result,
data in
    if let image = UIImage(data: data) {
      result.append(image)
    }
  }
}
```

Don't be put off if the code doesn't speak to you at first. Like most modern concurrency APIs, this example is both your first encounter with TaskGroup and almost everything you need to know about it.

Step by step, this code does the following:

1. You set each task's return type as Data via the of argument. The group as a whole will return [UIImage]. You could also have an explicit return type in the closure declaration and skip the returning argument.

2. Elsewhere in your code, you've calculated the number of images you want to fetch, which lets you loop through them here.

3. group is the ready-to-go ThrowingTaskGroup. Inside the for loop, you use group.addTask { ... } to add tasks to the group.

4. You perform the actual work of the task by fetching data from an API.

5. Task groups conform to your old friend AsyncSequence, so as each task in the group completes, you collect the results into an array of images and return it.

Long story short, the example starts a variable number of concurrent tasks, and each one downloads an image. Finally, you assign the array with all the images to images. Those few lines of code really pack quite a punch!

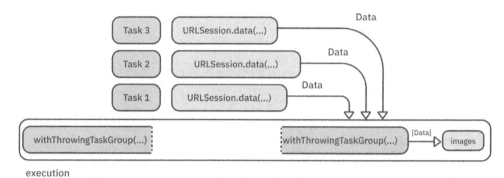

execution

You manage the group's tasks with the following APIs:

- **addTask(priority:operation:)**: Adds a task to the group for concurrent execution with the given (optional) priority.

- **addTaskUnlessCancelled(priority:operation:)**: Identical to addTask(...), except that it does nothing if the group is already canceled.

- **cancelAll()**: Cancels the group. In other words, it cancels all currently running tasks, along with all tasks added in the future.

- **isCancelled**: Returns true if the group is canceled.

- **isEmpty**: Returns true if the group has completed all its tasks, or has no tasks to begin with.

- **waitForAll()**: Waits until all tasks have completed. Use it when you need to execute some code after finishing the group's work.

As you see, TaskGroup conforms to AsyncSequence, so you can iterate over the group asynchronously to get the task return values, just like a regular Swift Sequence.

This is quite an ingenious design because it both runs concurrent tasks and iterates over the results as a sequence — and, therefore, in a non-concurrent context. That allows you to update your mutable state safely — for example, by storing the result of each task in an array.

In the next section, you'll try many of these great APIs in an app that searches for aliens.

# Getting started with Sky

In this chapter, you'll work on an iOS app called **Sky** that scans satellite imagery of the sky and analyzes it for signs of alien life.

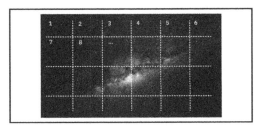

You'll scan the numbered sectors in a satellite image independently from each other. This allows you to use `TaskGroup` and perform many of these scans in parallel.

**Note**: The app will only *pretend* to scan the images. The goal of this chapter is to walk you through using concurrent task groups. If you're interested in *really* searching for alien life, check out The SETI Institute (https://bit.ly/3C4k62y).

As with other projects in the book, **Sky** consists of a single screen already built for you in SwiftUI. Most of your work will go into the app's model, which will spawn concurrent tasks and manage their execution.

To get started, open this chapter's starter project. Then, build and run it. You'll see the main app UI. It features three indicators that show the scheduled tasks, the current tasks-per-second ratio and the number of completed scans:

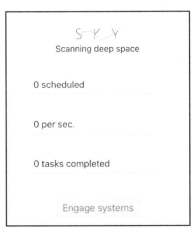

Tap the **Engage systems** button. The app will pop an alert telling you that it successfully scanned twenty sectors within zero seconds.

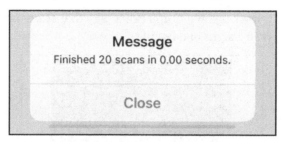

As you've already guessed, the app didn't *actually* perform anything. The button calls the starter code, but the model doesn't scan any data. That's why you get the record 0.00-second duration to complete the work.

The main points to note in the starter code are:

1.  The scanModel property in **Sky/SkyApp.swift** is the initialized model. It takes the number of tasks to perform in a single run and the name of the local device. You'll use that name in a later chapter.

2.  In **Sky/ScanModel.swift**, the three @Published properties that drive your UI are scheduled, countPerSecond and completed. onScheduled() and onTaskCompleted(), which you'll call from your own code later, manage those properties.

3.  Finally, peek in **Sky/Tasks/ScanTask.swift**. This is the type that "performs" a sky-sector scan. It takes an input, which is the number of the sector, and performs the actual work in run(). Luckily for your computer, run() only *simulates* hard work by blocking its thread for one second.

Now that you've had a quick walkthrough of the project, you'll move on to implementing the part of the model that runs the scans.

# Spawning tasks in a simple loop

Open **ScanModel.swift** and add the following convenience method anywhere inside the ScanModel class:

```
func worker(number: Int) async -> String {
  await onScheduled()

  let task = ScanTask(input: number)
  let result = await task.run()

  await onTaskCompleted()
  return result
}
```

This method not only runs a single task, but also tracks the execution in the model's state. Here's what this code does:

- Call onScheduled() to update the model counters. This method is annotated with @MainActor because it updates the UI. Updating the UI should always be a fast operation, so the await here won't affect the progress of the scanning task significantly.

- Create a new ScanTask with the given sector number.

- Wait for the results of the asynchronous call to run().

- Finally, call onTaskCompleted() to update the model counters and the app's UI on the main thread once again.

onScheduled() and onTaskCompleted() are both annotated with @MainActor to guarantee that updating the model counters, even from multiple copies of worker(number:) running in parallel, is safe.

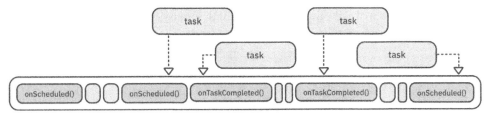

main thread

Next, scroll to runAllTasks(). The **Engage systems** button calls this method when you tap it. You'll add the code to perform concurrent scans here.

Now, add this code inside runAllTasks(). If you see a problem with the code, congratulate yourself, but indulge me and use it anyway:

```
var scans: [String] = []
for number in 0..<total {
  scans.append(await worker(number: number))
}
print(scans)
```

Here, you create an empty array called scans, then run a for loop to append the result of each scan task. Finally, you print the result to the console.

Build and run. Tap **Engage systems**; the indicators will liven up.

As the app progresses, you'll notice that there's always one scheduled task, and you're progressing at about one task per second.

If you've already noticed the flaw, this won't surprise you. You await the tasks *serially* inside the for loop instead of running in parallel. Finally, when the scan completes, the app shows a duration of just over twenty seconds.

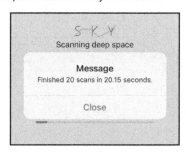

Each call to worker(number:) blocks the next one, regardless of whether the dispatcher uses one or more threads:

You need to work on multiple threads *at the same time* to perform concurrent work. You could do that manually by wrapping the code inside the loop in a Task. This would start all iterations immediately and at the same time.

But fear not, there's no need for manual labor. That's what the TaskGroup APIs do for you: launch tasks concurrently, track execution and, finally, collect the results.

# Creating a concurrent task group

Inside runAllTasks(), delete everything except the first line that resets started. Insert this instead:

```
await withTaskGroup(of: String.self) { [unowned self] group in

}
```

You use withTaskGroup(of:operation:) to create and run a task group. You also set each of the tasks to return a String. You'll call worker(number:) from inside the closure, so you capture self as an unowned reference.

Now, you can add some tasks to group by inserting this code in the withTaskGroup(...) closure:

```
for number in 0..<total {
  group.addTask {
    await self.worker(number: number)
  }
}
```

Here, you add a for loop like before, but this time you use addTask(priority:operation:) to add a task and swiftly move on to the next iteration of the loop.

Each task in the group calls worker(number:) and returns its result. This happens implicitly because you don't need to write return for single-line closures. At the moment, you don't collect the task results, but you will later in this chapter.

Build and run. Tap **Engage systems**. This time, you see the **Scheduled** indicator shoot straight up to twenty — and then nothing happens for a while. Finally, the jobs complete.

> **Note**: You'll see a different completion time depending on how many execution threads the system has made available to your app. In the screenshot above, the work finished in about 10 seconds, which means the app used two threads. If you see about 7 seconds, that's three threads, 5 seconds would be four, and so on. If you still see 20 seconds, you only had one execution thread available to do any work. In that case, try running the project on an iOS device rather than the simulator.

You'll deal with the lack of UI updates shortly, but something is definitely going right — the time it takes to complete all of the tasks dropped, meaning the app is now working concurrently!

The app has performed twenty seconds of work in ten seconds of actual time. This is your first hint that you're doing concurrency right — you're using more CPU time than the amount of astronomical time that's passed.

The duration is 50% shorter, and that means that the Swift runtime allotted two execution threads *at a time* from the thread-pool to your task group like so:

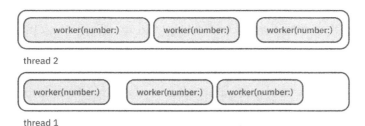

Because addTask(...) returns immediately, all twenty tasks are scheduled instantly, before the tasks start. The runtime then starts all the tasks, so the Scheduled indicator fills all the way up. Then, things start to go wrong. The work is being done, and being done concurrently, but you don't see any UI updates. Why is that?

## Controlling task execution

Remember that the concurrency system breaks operations down into partials. Resuming after an await is a partial, just like anything else. After the first ScanTask.run() completes, the concurrency system now has to choose between running a different scheduled scan task or resuming any of the completed ones.

> **Note**: If you need a quick refresher on partial tasks in Swift, take a moment to review the section called "Separating code into partial tasks" in Chapter 2, "Getting Started With async/await".

You haven't given the system any information about which option is more important, so it's doing what you asked it to do first — running the scans.

Your users are anxious for news of alien life! To make the concurrency system understand this, you need to tell it that scanning tasks are less important than updating the UI.

Open **Sky/Tasks/ScanTask.swift** and update run() to give the task a priority.

Replace:

```
await Task {
```

With:

```
await Task(priority: .medium) {
```

If you don't set a priority, the task will get the priority of its parent. In this case, that priority is .userInitiated because the original task started from the main thread.

With this change, you give the scanning task a lower priority — medium, in this case. That means the scheduler *should* (priorities are only suggestions) favor resuming after a completed scan over beginning the next one. Since UI updates are super quick, this won't keep you from the aliens for too long.

Keep in mind that changing the priority here will *not make* tasks run faster or slower. It just bumps the UI tasks toward the front of the executor queue instead of appending them after all of the scan tasks.

Build and run. Tap **Engage systems**. Now, you'll see the completed progress fill up in real time:

With that wrinkle out of the way, you can return to figuring out if you found any alien life during this particular scan.

# Getting results from a task group

An important detail to note about withTaskGroup is that it waits for all tasks to finish before returning. That means that, on the next line of code after calling this function, it's safe to assume all the tasks have completed.

"But where is the *result* of the group execution?" you might ask. Since you don't explicitly return a value from withTaskGroup(...)'s trailing closure, the function returns no value (i.e., Void).

As you briefly touched upon earlier in the chapter, TaskGroup and ThrowingTaskGroup expose their results via an AsyncSequence conformance. In other words, you can use everything you already know about asynchronous sequences to iterate over the task results in group.

Open **ScanModel.swift** and scroll to runAllTasks(). At the end of the task group closure, after the for loop, add the following code:

```
return await group
  .reduce(into: [String]()) { result, string in
    result.append(string)
  }
```

You use reduce(into:block:), inherited from AsyncSequence, to collect all the returned task values and collect them in an array.

The compiler will promptly complain about this change. To fix that, update the line that creates the task group to add a closure return type and assign the result to a local variable, like so:

```
let scans = await withTaskGroup(
  of: String.self
) { [unowned self] group -> [String] in
```

This will clear the compiler error and also assign the group result to scans. To verify the group results, add the following **at the end** of the runAllTasks() method:

```
print(scans)
```

Build and run one more time. Tap **Engage systems** and, once the scanning completes, look at Xcode's output console. You'll see the values returned by the group:

```
["1", "0", "2", "3", "4", "5", "6", "7", "9", "10", "8", "11",
 "13", "12", "15", "14", "16", "17", "18", "19"]
```

Note how the numbers aren't sorted in increasing order. `TaskGroup` executes tasks in the order it finds fitting to optimize system resources.

Additionally, tasks with higher priority will execute before tasks with lower priority, regardless of the order you add them.

# Mutating shared state

A final point to make about using task groups is that it's quite important to understand which parts of your code actually run **in parallel**.

By design, you can return any results of the concurrent execution from the task and safely collect those results by iterating over the group. However, sometimes you need to update some kind of shared state directly from inside a group task.

For example, concurrent tasks that download a file from a server might log the result immediately via a shared app logger object. This way, if one of the files fails to download and the request throws an error, the rest of the requests will still log successfully as soon as they get the file:

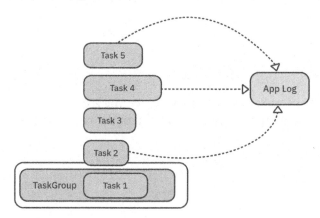

If you end up mutating shared state — like an instance property or a top-level variable — concurrently, you'll create a data race that might eventually crash your app. A data race occurs when multiple threads access the same data in memory, and at least one of them is trying to modify that data:

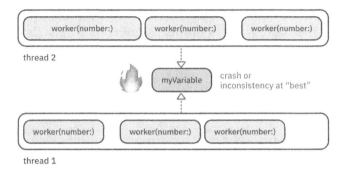

The tricky part about data races is that you *almost never* experience a crash when you run your app in debug mode from Xcode. Data races most often produce crashes when you compile an app to release and run it on a device. And as luck has it, it's bound to happen more often to your end users than to you as a developer.

Long story short, you need to be vigilant about which parts of your task group code run concurrently and avoid modifying the shared state from within that group. The completed group code roughly splits across concurrent, asynchronous and synchronous execution, like so:

```
let scans = await withTaskGroup(of: String.self) { [unowned self] group -> [String] in
  for number in 0..<total {                    asynchronous
    group.addTask {
      await self.worker(number: number)
    }                           concurrent
  }
  return await group
    .reduce(into: [String]()) { result, string in
      result.append(string)
    }                                  asynchronous
}
print(scans)  synchronous
```

- It's **mostly safe** to modify shared state from the synchronous parts of the code (in green) — for example, from outside the task group.

- It's **somewhat safe** to modify state from asynchronous parts (in orange), if the compiler doesn't complain. But to do that, you have to be sure you aren't introducing a data race.

- It's **dangerous** to modify state from the concurrent parts (in red), unless you use a safety mechanism.

Luckily, the new concurrency model also provides a new API to make your concurrent code safe. You'll learn about it in detail in Chapter 8, "Getting Started With Actors".

At the moment, your group churns through all its tasks and eventually ends up with a result. But what if you were to actually find alien life? Wouldn't you want to do something about that right away? In the next section, you'll learn how to handle task results as they come in.

## Processing task results in real time

Sometimes, you need to run a bunch of concurrent tasks and simply use the collected results at the end of the job, just as you implemented `runAllTasks()` in the previous section.

In other situations, you need to react immediately to each task's result. For example, you might want to update the UI to show progress or control the group execution flow depending on the task's results.

Luckily, `TaskGroup` allows you to **dynamically** manage the workload of the group. You can cancel tasks, add new tasks during execution and more.

> **Note**: This is an important distinction to make for readers who are used to the older Grand Central Dispatch API, `DispatchQueue.concurrentPerform(iterations:execute:)`, which didn't allow any control over the execution.

In the previous section, you collected the results and returned a value from `withTaskGroup`. Now, you'll remove the `return` and process the results inside the closure.

Open **ScanModel.swift**, if you don't already have it onscreen, and remove this entire `return` statement from the closure in `runAllTasks()`:

```
return try await group
  .reduce(into: [String]()) { result, string in
    result.append(string)
  }
```

To satisfy the compiler, change the task group creation code to account for the lack of return value:

```
await withTaskGroup(of: String.self) { [unowned self] group in
```

Then remove this line, as well:

```
print(scans)
```

Now — on to the new code. At the bottom of `withTaskGroup`'s closure, after the `for` loop, append this:

```
for await result in group {
  print("Completed: \(result)")
}
print("Done.")
```

`group` conforms to `AsyncSequence` so you can comfortably iterate its results in a loop.

The loop runs as long as there are pending tasks and suspends before each iteration. It ends when the group finishes running all its tasks.

Build and run. Tap **Engage systems** and observe the output console. You'll see something like:

```
...
Completed: 13
Completed: 14
Completed: 15
Completed: 17
Completed: 16
Completed: 19
Completed: 18
Done.
```

The runtime executes the tasks asynchronously. As soon as each task completes, the `for await` loop runs one more time.

Next, you'll look into gaining even more control over the group execution by using custom iteration logic.

# Controlling the group flow

As mentioned earlier in the chapter, the TaskGroup APIs are very flexible, largely thanks to their simplicity. This section will show you how to combine these simple APIs to compose a more complex behavior.

Right now, you schedule all the tasks and let the runtime decide how many to execute and when, until it exhausts the tasks in the group. This, however, might not always be what you want to do.

Scanning for signs of alien life requires plenty of heavy work that might strain the device. In this section, you'll restrict the concurrent task group to execute **no more than four tasks** at the same time, making sure the Sky app never overloads your system.

Scroll to runAllTasks() in **ScanModel.swift**, if you don't have it open at the moment.

To make space for new code, **replace** all of the code inside withTaskGroup(...)'s closure with:

```
let batchSize = 4

for index in 0..<batchSize {
  group.addTask {
    await self.worker(number: index)
  }
}
```

Here, you define a batch size of four tasks to run concurrently, then start exactly four of them in your group.

You still have sixteen more to run to complete the work. You'll cover those by adding a new task to the group **each time** a previous task completes.

Insert this directly below the last code:

```
// 1
var index = batchSize

// 2
for await result in group {
  print("Completed: \(result)")
  // 3
  if index < total {
    group.addTask { [index] in
      await self.worker(number: index)
```

```
      }
      index += 1
    }
  }
}
```

In this code, you:

1.  Define a starting index and set it to the batch size.

2.  Loop over any completing tasks and print "Completed ...".

3.  Then, as long as the current index is less than the total number of tasks, you add one more task to the group.

This is a fine example of how flexible the task group APIs are in reality. Namely:

*   You iterate over the results **and** add fresh tasks at the same time.

*   You control **how many** tasks can run at the same time.

*   Last but not least, you don't need to change anything outside `withTaskGroup(...)` because these logic changes are **completely transparent** to the consumer.

Adding tasks to a group while it's running allows you to do many interesting things, including (but not limited) to:

*   Keeping a group running indefinitely by always adding more and more tasks.

*   Retrying tasks by re-adding them to the group upon failure.

*   Inserting a high-priority UI task after either a set number of computational tasks finish running or you find a given result.

With these fresh ideas in mind, build and run. Tap **Engage systems**.

This time, the scan indicators paint a different picture:

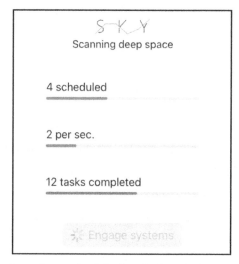

You continuously remain at four scheduled tasks because, as soon as one completes, you schedule a new one in its place.

The second indicator, however, shows that you advance the total amount of work by only two (or however many you saw before) tasks per second. That matches what you established earlier in the chapter — namely, that the Swift runtime "gives" your group a device-specific number of threads to run concurrent tasks on.

Congratulations, your new concurrent code works exactly as expected!

# Running code after all tasks have completed

Oftentimes you'd like to do some cleanup, update the UI or do something else after you run a group.

In your current project, you'd like to reset some indicators to not confuse the user when the scan is over.

You could always use `TaskGroup.waitForAll()` to wait on all the tasks, then add the cleanup code.

But in your current `runAllTasks()` implementation, you already wait for all the tasks to complete. As mentioned, the `for await` loop will only end when the group runs out of tasks.

So all you need to do is to add this code directly after the last loop in
runAllTasks():

```
await MainActor.run {
  completed = 0
  countPerSecond = 0
  scheduled = 0
}
```

This sets the three indicators in the UI to zero at the end of the scan.

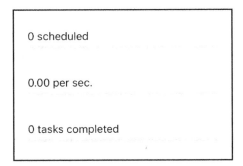

Easy! Now on to a more painful topic: error handling.

# Group error handling

So far, running scans has been a walk in the park. ScanTask never fails and always
completes its heavy-duty work on time.

That will change in this section! ScanTask.run() will fail now and then, and you'll
have to cope with the consequences.

Open **ScanTask.swift** and scroll to run(). First, make the method throwing by
adding the throws keyword to its definition:

```
func run() async throws -> String {
```

Thrown errors move upward toward the calling code. You'll need to track that path
back to fix the compiler errors, which will help you visualize where the errors go.
Before you leave, though, add this line at the top of the method:

```
try UnreliableAPI.action(failingEvery: 10)
```

The starter project includes UnreliableAPI, which simply throws an error every few
calls so you can test some error handling scenarios.

Now that you're producing errors, you need to handle them. The code that calls run() now fails to compile because it's not using the try keyword.

Open **ScanModel.swift** and fix the compiler error in worker(number:) by adding try:

```
let result = try await task.run()
```

The next step is to modify the declaration of worker(number:) to also include throws:

```
func worker(number: Int) async throws -> String {
```

Then, scroll to runAllTasks() and add try to the two calls to worker(number:):

```
try await self.worker(number: index)
```

You now have throwing tasks, so you have to update the task group to also be a throwing one. Update the group creation call with the throwing variant withThrowingTaskGroup like so:

```
try await withThrowingTaskGroup(of: String.self) { [unowned
self] group in
```

Finally, group is now a ThrowingTaskGroup, so you must also update the for await loop :

```
for try await result in group {
```

The project now compiles once more. Build and run. Tap **Engage systems** and observe the app. Right around the time you see the completed task indicator go up to ten, the execution stops:

You don't catch errors anywhere in your model, so the error bubbles up and out of the group. The starter code in **SkyApp.swift** catches the error and presents it on-screen.

The result of this behavior is that, when one of your tasks throws, it "breaks" the whole group. Not only do further tasks not execute, you also don't get the results of the ones that have already completed.

In the next section, you'll redesign your code to ignore failing tasks and to collect the results of all the tasks that successfully return.

# Using the Result type with TaskGroup

To handle errors safely, you won't throw an error; instead, you'll use the `Result` type. If you haven't used `Result` before, it's a simple Swift enum with the following two cases:

- **success(Value)**: With an associated result.

- **failure(Error)**: With an associated error.

Open **ScanModel.swift** and scroll to `worker(number:)` and change the method definition to avoid throwing errors and return a `Result` value instead:

```
func worker(number: Int) async -> Result<String, Error> {
```

This upsets the compiler. To make it happy again, start by replacing `return result` with:

```
return .success(result)
```

Then, replace the throwing line `let result = try await task.run()` with:

```
let result: String
do {
  result = try await task.run()
} catch {
  return .failure(error)
}
```

Here, you call `run()`, as you did before. But this time, you catch any errors and safely return `failure` instead.

Changing the return type threw some other compiler errors, which you'll now fix.

In `runAllTasks()`, you need to change the group return type from `String` to `Result<String, Error>`. Make that change on the line of `withThrowingTaskGroup(of: String.self)` so it looks like this:

```
withThrowingTaskGroup(of: Result<String, Error>.self)
```

That changes the group to expect a `Result` from each task; it also clears the compile errors. However, some warnings are still left, so you need to change the two occurrences of `try await self.worker(number: index)` back to:

```
await self.worker(number: index)
```

Sweet! Build and run. Tap **Engage systems**. Now, the app works through all the tasks, skipping over any that fail.

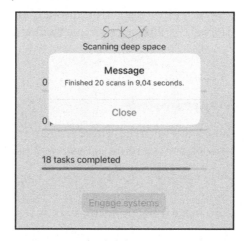

Note how the alert box says you worked through 20 scan tasks, but the lowest indicator shows that 18 tasks actually finished. The difference between the two results is the number of tasks that failed.

Now, you only need to take care of the logs. Right now, you print the raw `Result` description, which is a bit untidy:

```
Completed: success("5")
Completed: success("7")
Completed: success("6")
Completed: failure(Sky.UnreliableAPI.Error())
Completed: success("8")
Completed: success("10")
```

Scroll to print("Completed: \(result)") and replace it with:

```
switch result {
case .success(let result):
  print("Completed: \(result)")
case .failure(let error):
  print("Failed: \(error.localizedDescription)")
}
```

Build and run. Scan again, and you will have a nicer looking log:

```
Completed: 5
Completed: 6
Completed: 7
Failed: UnreliableAPI.action(failingEvery:) failed.
Completed: 10
Completed: 8
Completed: 12
```

And that's a wrap! You've now learned a ton about using TaskGroup and its flexibility and power.

But your search for alien life isn't over! In Chapter 10, "Actors in a Distributed System", you'll increase your scanning power by adding new code to Sky to allow it to take over other devices on the network. This means it will perform its scans in a sort of... **SkyNet**. I'm sure "you'll be back" to read that one!

# Key points

- To run an arbitrary number of concurrent tasks, create a **task group**. Do this by using the function withTaskGroup(of:returning:body:). For a throwing task group, use withThrowingTaskGroup(of:returning:body:).

- You can **add tasks** to a group by calling addTask(priority:operation:) or addTaskUnlessCancelled(priority:operation:).

- Control task execution by **canceling the group** via cancelAll() or **waiting for all tasks to complete** with waitForAll().

- Use the group as an **asynchronous sequence** to iterate over each task result in real time.

# Chapter 8: Getting Started With Actors

By Marin Todorov

In the last chapter, you used the `TaskGroup` and `ThrowingTaskGroup` APIs to execute tasks in parallel, allowing you to make use of multiple threads and CPU cores on your device. This boosts your app's performance and allows you to run more satellite scans in the same amount of time as non-task-group code.

You explored `TaskGroup`'s ingenious design, which allows you to run tasks **in parallel** but still collect the execution's results in a safe, **serial** manner by iterating the group as an asynchronous sequence.

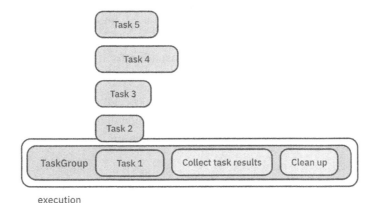

execution

As mentioned in the "Mutating shared state" subsection of the previous chapter, some problems require you to update your state from a concurrent context. That's one of the challenging aspects of concurrent programming: taming different threads that try to access the same piece of memory at the same time.

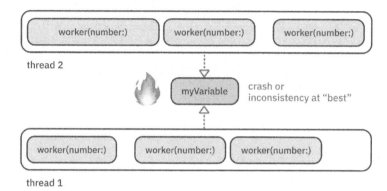

This chapter will cover how the new Swift concurrency model addresses data races by using a new type: **actor**.

Before you dive into this new type, you'll take a moment to understand what the issue with updating mutable state *really* is.

# Understanding thread-safe code

You might have seen methods described as **thread-safe** in documentation from Apple or third-party frameworks.

This usually means that, regardless of whether you're calling an API from the main thread or a so-called background thread, the method will always behave as expected. In other words, the method will still work, even when multiple threads call it at the same time.

> **Note:** The concept of thread-safe code is also sometimes referred to as *linearizability* or *atomicity*, which aims to limit the outcomes of concurrently accessing an object from multiple processes.

Unfortunately, in Objective-C and versions of Swift before 5.5, there was no syntax to mark a method as thread-safe. You had to rely on each method's documentation to find out whether it was safe or not.

Third-party frameworks sometimes give you access to their source, but that doesn't always solve the problem. For example, can you tell immediately if this piece of code is thread-safe?

```swift
class Counter {
  private var count = 0

  func increment() {
    count += 1
  }
}
```

As you see, nothing stands out when you look at `Counter` that would make it particularly *unsafe*.

And yet, if two threads running in parallel both call `Counter.increment()`, you might not end up with a `count` increased by exactly two. Even worse, if the two calls to `Counter.increment()` happen at *precisely* the same moment — your app will crash.

Even more worrisome is that crashes rarely happen when you compile your app for debugging — for example, when the app is running in your iOS simulator or you started it from Xcode on your device. Release builds are the ones that are optimized and fast enough to produce a data-race crash.

Therefore, you can say that *any code* that doesn't take proactive steps towards protecting shared mutable state from concurrent access is inherently **not thread-safe**.

Before Swift 5.5, developers used **locks** or **serial dispatch queues** to ensure exclusive access to shared state. With a lock, for example, a thread locks the access to a shared resource, and other threads need to wait for it to unlock before they can read or write to that same resource.

Effectively, threads lock each other out to guarantee exclusive access to the resource:

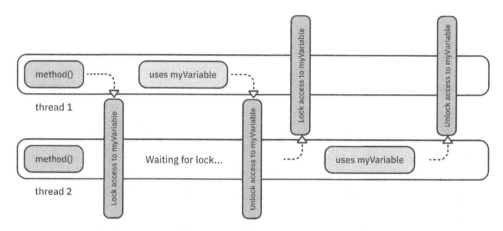

Concurrent code that uses lock APIs — like `os_unfair_lock` — is fairly fast and safe when written well. The previous code sample looks like this when you use a lock:

```
class Counter {
  private var lock = os_unfair_lock_s()
  private var count = 0

  func increment() {
    os_unfair_lock_lock(&lock)
    count += 1
    os_unfair_lock_unlock(&lock)
  }
}
```

Aside from its relative verbosity, the code looks pretty straightforward. It's a viable solution to protecting `count`.

However, do you remember why you looked into this section's code sample in the first place? As a developer using this API, how can you tell if calling `Counter.increment()` is thread-safe or not? Furthermore, how can the compiler itself know your code is thread-safe, so it can help protect you from any races resulting from a developer mistake, for example?

If you don't have access to the code, or the free time to read it thoroughly, there's really no way to tell if it's really safe. That's where actors come in.

# Meeting actor

The **actor type** is one of the concurrency-related improvements introduced in Swift 5.5. actor is a programming type just like its peers: enum, struct, class and so on. More specifically, it's a reference type like class.

The code looks quite familiar, too. Here's the example from the previous section. This time, however, it replaces class with actor to make it thread-safe:

```
actor Counter {
  private var count = 0

  func increment() {
    count += 1
  }
}
```

You might wonder if a new language type is really necessary to address data races. In this and the next chapters, you'll explore many of actor's specific behaviors. You'll discover for yourself that actors are both complex and powerful — and certainly a type-worthy addition to Swift.

Actors are an existing, well-established **model for concurrent computation**. You can read about them in detail in Wikipedia's Actor model (https://en.wikipedia.org/wiki/Actor_model) article.

Actors behave according to a few basic rules that allow them to guarantee the safety of their internal state. Different implementations vary across languages, so in this chapter, you'll learn how actors function *specifically* in Swift.

An actor in Swift can safely access and mutate its own state. A special type called a **serial executor**, which the runtime manages, synchronizes all calls to the actor's members. The serial executor, much like a serial dispatch queue in GCD, executes tasks one after another. By doing this, it protects the actor's state from concurrent access:

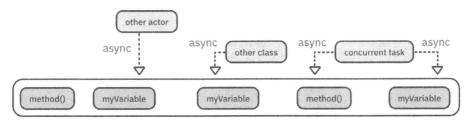

actor serial executor

When you look up the `Actor` protocol (https://developer.apple.com/documentation/swift/actor), which all actors adhere to, you'll see there's only a single requirement. Namely, all actors must have a property called `unownedExecutor`, which is the aforementioned executor that serializes access to the actor state.

But what about the real cause of data races? How can you guarantee another type won't call your actor from multiple threads at the same time and cause a crash?

`actor` has a special deal with the Swift compiler to take care of that.

Access to the actor from other types is automatically performed asynchronously and scheduled on the actor's serial executor. This is called the **state isolation layer**, outlined here:

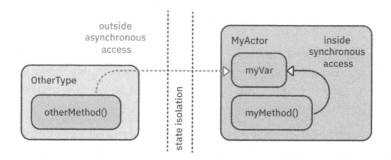

The state isolation layer ensures that all state mutation is **thread-safe**. `actor` itself is the guarantee of thread-safety for consumers of the API, the compiler and the runtime.

# Recognizing the main actor

You've already worked with actors in this book, although they were only mentioned in passing. Any time you had to work on UI-related code, you ran it on the **main actor**.

You ran code on the main actor by calling `MainActor.run(...)`. Additionally, you annotated methods that should automatically run on the main actor with `@MainActor`.

Is the main actor an `actor` type with all of the actor behaviors discussed above?

Yes, indeed! The main actor runs code serially on the main thread and protects its shared state: the UI of your app. It's a **global actor** that's accessible from anywhere, and you can use its **shared instance** across your app.

You'll learn more about global actors in Chapter 9, "Global Actors".

Now that you've praised the main actor for its stellar performance in your app's architecture, it's time to get started with this chapter's project — implementing your first actor types.

# Getting started with actors

**EmojiArt** is an app that lets you browse an online catalog of digital emoji art. To verify that the digital art is authentic, the app reads the feed of current works of art from the server, verifies the digital signature of the images and, only then, displays them onscreen.

Open the starter version of EmojiArt in this chapter's materials, under **projects/starter**.

Like all projects in this book, EmojiArt's SwiftUI views, navigation and data models are already wired up and ready to go. This app has more code than this book's other projects, but you'll use it to work through a lot of concepts throughout this and the next chapters.

> **Note**: Like the rest of this book's projects, EmojiArt uses sample data to teach a set of concepts; it's not an actual digital art store.

You use an actor when you want to protect a state from concurrent mutation. You'll try out actors for the first time by implementing the app's loading screen.

You'll display a live-updating progress bar of the feed's verification process and use an actor to safely update the progress value from concurrently running tasks.

Before getting started with the project, start the book server. If you haven't already done that, navigate to the server folder **00-book-server** in the book materials-repository and enter swift run. The detailed steps are covered in Chapter 1, "Why Modern Swift Concurrency?".

Now, build and run the project. Take a look at EmojiArt's initial state:

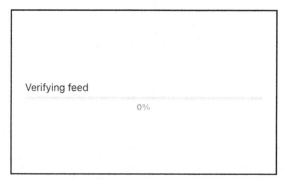

Here, you see LoadingView, which will run the verification onscreen. Once that's done, the app will navigate to ListView, which displays the actual art pieces.

You haven't implemented the model method that verifies the images yet, so the progress bar is stuck at zero percent with no chance of completion. You'll fix that as you work through this chapter.

# Mutating state concurrently

Open the app's model file, **EmojiArtModel.swift**, and add this new code inside the class:

> **Note**: If you already ran the app, you'll see a warning about updating the UI from a background thread. Ignore it for now; you'll fix it shortly.

```
private(set) var verifiedCount = 0

func verifyImages() async throws {
  try await withThrowingTaskGroup(of: Void.self) { group in

  }
}
```

verifiedCount is the verification counter that you'll update concurrently. verifyImages() is the method that will verify the individual pieces of artwork. To perform concurrent work, you create a new task group via withThrowingTaskGroup(...), as you did in the previous chapter.

Unlike before, however, you'll update your state *directly* from the task body so that mutation happens **concurrently** and in **real time**.

To perform the verification, insert the following code inside withThrowingTaskGroup(...)'s trailing closure:

```
imageFeed.forEach { file in
  group.addTask { [unowned self] in
    try await Checksum.verify(file.checksum)
    self.verifiedCount += 1
  }
}

try await group.waitForAll()
```

In the code above, you iterate over the image files in `imageFeed`, assuming the model has already fetched those from the server, and add a new task for each file. If `Checksum.verify(_:)` detects an asset with an invalid checksum, it throws an error. Otherwise, the asset is valid and you increase `verifiedCount` by one.

Finally, you use `group.waitForAll()` to wait for all tasks to complete and re-throw any task errors out of the group.

> **Note**: As you know, the group implicitly waits for its tasks to complete before returning. However, if you don't use any `try` keywords inside the group closure, the compiler decides you want a non-throwing group and will not re-throw task errors! To fix this, you use `waitForAll()` prefixed with `try` to hint to the compiler that it should use a throwing group after all.

Given all your experience with these book's projects, you're likely already rolling your eyes because you know that mutating `verifiedCount` from within the task is unsafe. No worries, you'll fix that in a moment.

## Showing the art and updating the progress

You'll start by adding a call to `verifyImages(...)` in the screen showing the verification indicator. Open **LoadingView.swift** and scroll to the `task { ... }` view modifier.

Just below `try await model.loadImages()` — the line that fetches the image feed from the server — insert:

```
try await model.verifyImages()
withAnimation {
   isVerified = true
}
```

After successfully fetching the feed, you call `verifyImages()` to verify the authenticity of the assets. Finally, you set `isVerified` to `true`. Changing `isVerified` causes the main view to replace `LoadingView` with `ListView` and display the image feed onscreen.

Build and run. You'll see that, shortly after displaying LoadingView, the image feed pops up. The thumbnails aren't visible right now, but you can see the names and prices of the works of art.

Since you update verifiedCount concurrently and want to avoid overwhelming the main thread, you'll add a timer to LoadingView that will periodically update the progress bar during verification.

Add this new view modifier to LoadingView, just below where the alert modifier code wraps up:

```
.onReceive(timer) { _ in
  guard !model.imageFeed.isEmpty else { return }

  progress = Double(model.verifiedCount) /
Double(model.imageFeed.count)
}
```

The starter code for LoadingView includes a ready-to-go timer property called timer. In onReceive(_:perform:), you subscribe to this timer and make sure there are actually feed items, to avoid unnecessary updates.

Finally, you divide the number of verified assets by the count of all images, then update progress. This will update the progress bar with the latest value a few times per second.

Build and run one more time. You'll now see the verification go through to one hundred percent.

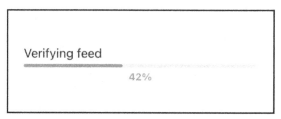

Surprisingly, everything seems to be running just fine with *no crashes*, despite the concurrent updates.

So *are there* any race conditions in the code you just wrote? It's quite hard to tell, considering the app is compiled for debugging and doesn't have any optimizations. This might mean the app is just *too slow* to reproduce this scenario, compared to an optimized release version that is more prone to triggering a data race.

# Detecting race conditions

One way to detect data races in your code is to enable the **Thread Sanitizer** in your Xcode project scheme. Click the scheme selector in Xcode's toolbar and select **Edit scheme…**:

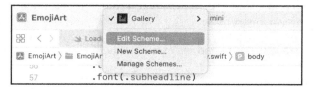

Next, in the scheme window, click **Run**, then select the **Diagnostics** tab. Check the **Thread Sanitizer** checkbox and, finally, close the scheme editing window.

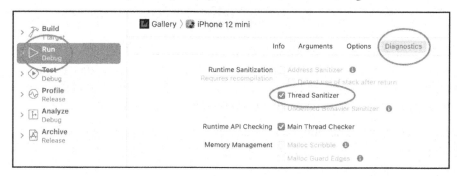

When you rebuild the project, Xcode will bake some extra checks into your app. At runtime, these will verify whether your code concurrently mutates any data.

Build and run. Let the app load and switch to the feed screen.

The app UI looks the same as before. If you direct your attention to Xcode, however, you'll notice a new purple runtime warning:

```
▼ 🟦 EmojiArt - 45256 1 issue              73   func verifyImages() async throws {
  ▼ ⚠ Threading Issues                     74     return try await
    ▼ ! Swift access race in (1) await     75       withThrowingTaskGroup(of: Void.self) { group in
        resume partial function for        76         imageFeed.forEach { file in
        closure #1 @Sendable () asy...     77           group.addTask { [unowned self] in
        ⊕ Location is a 40-byte heap       78             try await Checksum.verify(file.checksum)
          object at 0x7b0c00050760         79             self.verifiedCount += 1  ⚠ Swift access race in (1) await resume partial function
        > ⚫ Mutating access by threa...    80           }
        > ⚫ Mutating access by threa...    81         }
        > ⚫ Heap block allocated by t...   82
                                           83         try await group.waitForAll()
                                           84       }
```

If Thread Sanitizers detects a data race, the code will eventually crash in production. This is *no bueno*.

# Using actors to protect shared mutable state

To protect `EmojiArtModel.verifiedCount` from concurrent access, you'll convert `EmojiArtModel` from a class to an actor. Since actors exhibit a lot of typical class behavior, such as by-reference semantics, the change shouldn't be too complex.

Open **EmojiArtModel.swift** and replace `class EmojiArtModel: ObservableObject` with:

```
actor EmojiArtModel: ObservableObject
```

This changes the type of the model to an actor. Your shared state is now safe!

As you see in Xcode, actors don't magically solve concurrent access — you're now facing a compile error. The compiler now follows the rules for actors and finds issues in the code that used to compile before.

In other words, some of your code that used to work **doesn't compile** as an actor. The compiler doesn't magically solve the issues; instead, it **suggests how you should change** your code to make it work safely in a concurrent context. But more importantly, when you use an actor, the compiler **protects** you against creating unsafe thread accesses in your code.

Now, you'll follow Xcode's directions to make the existing code thread-safe.

The error says:

```
"Actor-isolated property 'verifiedCount' can not be mutated from
a Sendable closure".
```

You'll learn about `Sendable` in the next sections. For now, just know you get the error because you can't update the actor state from "outside" of its direct scope.

This chapter's introduction mentioned that all code that **isn't confined to the serial executor** of the actor is "outside" access. That means it includes calls from other types and concurrent tasks — like your `TaskGroup`, in this case.

To overcome this issue, you'll extract the code to increment `verifiedCount` into a method, then call it asynchronously. This allows the actor to serialize the calls to that method.

Add this new method anywhere inside `EmojiArtModel`:

```
private func increaseVerifiedCount() {
  verifiedCount += 1
}
```

As discussed before, you can call this method synchronously from "inside" the actor's direct scope, but the compiler will **enforce asynchronous access** from "outside" of it.

Now, find `self.verifiedCount += 1` in your concurrent task code. Replace it with:

```
await self.increaseVerifiedCount()
```

This new code will make calls to `increaseVerifiedCount()` serially; this ensures you mutate your shared state safely.

Sadly, once you resolve that error, you still face a whole bunch of compiler errors. Now that `imageFeed` is part of your `EmojiArtModel` actor, you can't access that property on the main actor. *Oh, the terror!* SwiftUI runs on the main actor and can't read the feed anymore. You'll fix that next.

## Sharing data across actors

Given that you mostly use `EmojiArtModel.imageFeed` to drive the app's UI, it makes sense to place this property on the main actor. But how can you **share** it between the main actor and `EmojiArtModel`?

In this section, you'll move `imageFeed` to execute on the main actor, but the property itself will remain inside `EmojiArtModel`. It sounds a bit *esoteric*, but it's actually straightforward. In fact, **you've already done it** many times in this book — by using the `@MainActor` attribute.

Open **EmojiArtModel.swift** and scroll to `imageFeed`. Annotate the property with `@MainActor`, so it looks like this:

```
@Published @MainActor private(set) var imageFeed: [ImageFile] =
[]
```

This code moves `imageFeed` from the `EmojiArtModel`'s serial executor to the main actor. That clears the compile errors in the SwiftUI code because `imageFeed` is now accessible from the main thread.

To fix the rest of the errors, replace `imageFeed.removeAll()` in `loadImages()` with:

```
await MainActor.run {
  imageFeed.removeAll()
}
```

And replace `imageFeed = list` with:

```
await MainActor.run {
  imageFeed = list
}
```

The new code makes a little detour from running code on your actor's executor. Instead, it runs the two calls asynchronously on the main actor, where it's safe to update the UI:

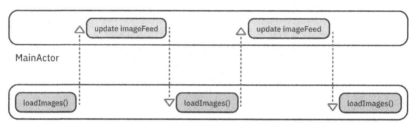

You've now fixed almost all the errors; you'll take care of the rest next.

## Fixing the remaining errors

Scroll to `verifyImages()` and find the error on the line that calls `imageFeed.forEach { ... }`. To access the actor, you need to call `imageFeed.forEach { ... }` asynchronously. Prepend an `await` before the call, like this:

```
await imageFeed.forEach { file in
```

There's one final error left in **LoadingView.swift**. Toward the bottom of the file, there's an error on the line that calculates the value of `progress`:

```
Actor-isolated property 'verifiedCount' can not be referenced
from the main actor
```

Prepend the math expression with an await and wrap the offending line in a Task, like so:

```
Task {
  progress = await Double(model.verifiedCount) /
    Double(model.imageFeed.count)
}
```

Congratulations, you've followed Xcode's guidance to completion and fixed all the unsafe code. Build and run again. This time, there aren't any purple warnings!

At this point in the chapter, you've worked through designing your first actor type and experienced some actor-specific compiler behavior. But there's one topic you skipped over: What is the Sendable type that those compiler errors mentioned? You'll learn about Sendable next.

# Understanding Sendable

Sendable is a protocol that indicates that a given value is **safe to use in concurrent code**. "Use how?" you might ask. Dig in and see.

Open the Sendable protocol's documentation page ([https://developer.apple.com/documentation/swift/sendable](https://developer.apple.com/documentation/swift/sendable)).

Scroll down a bit to the **Inherited By** section, and you'll see that a few protocols inherit from Sendable. For example, the Actor protocol is a Sendable; therefore, actor instances are safe to use in concurrent code. That makes sense.

In the next section, **Conforming Types**, you'll see that many types in Swift are sendable by default; for example: Bool, Double, Int, StaticString, UnsafePointer and others are all safe to use in concurrent code.

Generally speaking, value types are safe to use in concurrent code because value semantics prevent you from accidentally mutating a shared reference to the same object.

Classes are generally not sendable because their by-reference semantics allow you to **mutate the same instance in memory**. You did so earlier in this chapter, when you mutated verifiedCount on the same model instance concurrently.

You use the @Sendable attribute to **require thread-safe values** in your code. In other words, you use it to require that values must conform to the Sendable protocol.

For example, look at the Task type. Because it creates an asynchronous task that could unsafely mutate shared state, the Task.init(...) declaration **requires** that the operation closure is Sendable:

```
init(
  priority: TaskPriority? = nil,
  operation: @escaping @Sendable () async -> Success
)
```

The operation closure is @escaping because it's asynchronous and also @Sendable, which **verifies at compile-time** that the closure code is thread-safe. You already experienced this protection first-hand when you got compiler errors for trying to mutate shared state from inside TaskGroup.addTask(...).

To fully understand the role of the Sendable protocol, take a moment to have another look at its documentation page ([https://developer.apple.com/documentation/swift/sendable](https://developer.apple.com/documentation/swift/sendable)). Note how this protocol has *no requirements* — you really only use it to annotate types that you know are safe to use across threads.

Once you add Sendable conformance to one of your types, the compiler will automatically limit it in various ways to help you ensure its thread safety. For example, it'll ask you to make classes final, class properties immutable, and so on.

Look up addTask(...) and you'll see it also requires a Sendable closure:

```
mutating func addTask(
  priority: TaskPriority? = nil,
  operation: @escaping @Sendable () async -> ChildTaskResult
)
```

Therefore, the best practice in your own code is to require that any closures you run asynchronously be @Sendable, and that any values you use in asynchronous code adhere to the Sendable protocol.

Additionally, if your struct or class is thread-safe, you should also add Sendable conformance so other concurrent code can use it safely.

# Making safe methods nonisolated

Now that you've moved `imageFeed` off your own actor and onto the main actor, the methods that work with the feed don't actually work with your actor's shared state *directly*.

Back in **EmojiArtModel.swift**, scroll to `loadImages()` and check the code. None of it reads from or mutates either `imageFeed` or `verifiedCount`. You update `imageFeed` from the main actor, then the main actor serializes execution by default.

So in fact, `loadImages()` and `downloadImage(_:)` don't have *any state* to protect anymore. Therefore, they don't need the actor behavior at all.

When methods like that are safe, you can aid the runtime and remove the safety harness around them by marking them with the `nonisolated` keyword.

Prepend the `loadImages()` declaration with `nonisolated` like so:

```
nonisolated func loadImages() async throws
```

Next, do the same for `downloadImage(_:)`:

```
nonisolated func downloadImage(_ image: ImageFile) async throws
  -> Data
```

With these changes, the two methods behave as if they are vanilla **class** methods instead of **actor** methods. You also get a small performance win from removing the safety checks. You probably won't feel it if you call these methods a few times, but in a highly concurrent context, you'll see some speed improvement.

# Designing more complex actors

Now that you've created a fairly simple actor, it's time to try a more complex design. You'll mix actors, tasks and `async/await` to solve one of the eternal problems in programming: **image caching**.

Throughout the rest of the chapter, you'll build an actor that fetches the digital emoji assets from the book server and caches them in memory.

To start, add a new file to the project and call it **ImageLoader.swift**. Replace the placeholder code with the bare bones of that new actor:

```
import UIKit

actor ImageLoader {
  enum DownloadState {
    case inProgress(Task<UIImage, Error>)
    case completed(UIImage)
    case failed
  }

  private(set) var cache: [String: DownloadState] = [:]
}
```

In essence, this actor manages a cache dictionary that will store both the ongoing downloads and the images you've downloaded already.

cache contains values of type DownloadState, which can have one of these three download states:

- **inProgress**: The asset download has started but hasn't finished yet. This case gives you the **in-flight task**, which lets you await its completion and get the resulting image directly.

- **completed**: You've already downloaded the asset, and you're keeping the UIImage in memory.

- **failed**: You already tried downloading the asset with the given path, but the server returned an error.

## Filling up the cache

Next, you'll add a few methods to manage the cache: adding images, starting a new download and clearing the cache.

First, you'll use a method to add an image asset to the in-memory cache. Add this next method to your new actor:

```
func add(_ image: UIImage, forKey key: String) {
  cache[key] = .completed(image)
}
```

You can directly mutate cache from actor methods, so you simply set the value for the given asset key to .completed(image).

Next, you'll add a method to fetch a single image. It will get the image from memory if you've downloaded it already. Otherwise, it will get the image from the server. Start by checking the in-memory cache:

```
func image(_ serverPath: String) async throws -> UIImage {
  if let cached = cache[serverPath] {
    switch cached {
    case .completed(let image):
      return image
    case .inProgress(let task):
      return try await task.value
    case .failed: throw "Download failed"
    }
  }
}
```

If you find a value matching the asset key in `cache`, you use one of these three options:

- If the asset has finished downloading, you return the associated image.

- If the asset download is in progress, you await the associated task and return its `value`. This way, the original request will run as normal. The runtime will suspend here and return once the task completes.

- Finally, if the asset fails to download, you simply throw an error.

Next, it's time to add some code to download an image from the server if you don't find the asset in the local `cache`. Append the following code to the bottom of `image(_:)`:

```
let download: Task<UIImage, Error> = Task.detached {
  guard let url = URL(string: "http://
localhost:8080".appending(serverPath))
  else {
    throw "Could not create the download URL"
  }
  print("Download: \(url.absoluteString)")
  let data = try await URLSession.shared.data(from: url).0
  return try resize(data, to: CGSize(width: 200, height: 200))
}

cache[serverPath] = .inProgress(download)
```

Similar to previous chapters, you create a detached asynchronous task and download the image from the server. To keep track of the ongoing downloads, you print a debug log to the console.

Before returning, you call the starter-project function `resize(_:to:)` to scale down the server image and store it as a thumbnail.

Finally, once the task is ready, you add it to `cache` as an `inProgress` value. Should the same asset pop up in the feed again, you won't download it a second time. Instead, you'll wait for the ongoing `download` task to complete and return the fetched result.

## Wrapping up the image download

Last but not least, you need to handle the result of the download. Append this last piece of code to `image(_:)`:

```
do {
  let result = try await download.value
  add(result, forKey: serverPath)
  return result
} catch {
  cache[serverPath] = .failed
  throw error
}
```

Here, you wait for the download task to complete, then you call `add(_:forKey:)` to add the image to the in-memory cache and return it.

If the task throws, you update `cache` with a `failure` value for this asset before re-throwing the error.

With that, you've finished the actor's main logic. Before moving on, add one last convenience method to the actor:

```
func clear() {
  cache.removeAll()
}
```

You'll use `clear()` in the next chapter to clear the in-memory cache for debugging purposes.

Having finalized the new actor, you need to "spread the love" around your app so all the views can use it to display images.

# Sharing the actor

Since you'll use ImageLoader in a few different views, your next step is to inject it directly into the SwiftUI environment, so you can easily access it throughout your view hierarchy.

To use it as an environment object, though, you need to adhere to ObservableObject. Your loader doesn't feature any published properties, but SwiftUI requires an ObservableObject conformance anyway.

Open **ImageLoader.swift** and, at the top, add an ObservableObject conformance, like so:

```
actor ImageLoader: ObservableObject
```

Luckily, unlike other directions in this chapter, this change causes no compile errors. You can just move on with the next steps.

Open **AppMain.swift** and, under ListView(), add this modifier to inject the loader to the view hierarchy:

```
.environmentObject(ImageLoader())
```

Now, you can use ImageLoader from any view where you need images.

Another view bundled with the starter code, ThumbImage, displays a single asset in the image feed, so this is certainly a place where you'll need ImageLoader. Open **ThumbImage.swift** and add this new property to the type:

```
@EnvironmentObject var imageLoader: ImageLoader
```

This line initializes the injected image loader. You'll use it to fetch the asset image.

Move on to ThumbImage's view body, where you'll add one more modifier to start the thumbnail download. Directly after overlay(...), add:

```
.task {
  guard let image = try? await imageLoader.image(file.url) else
{
    overlay = "camera.metering.unknown"
    return
  }
  updateImage(image)
}
```

When the thumbnail view appears onscreen, you call `imageLoader.image(_:)` to fetch the image from the server. If the image has already been downloaded, you return the cached image instead.

If the download fails, you set an overlay for the thumbnail to show the user that the image load failed.

Finally, if everything was a success, you update the view image by calling `updateImage(_:)`.

Build and run. *At last*, you can enjoy some cool emoji art.

Wow, those "art" pieces aren't cheap!

> **Note**: If you want to "save" a few hundred dollars for an emoji art piece, you can peek into the book server's code and see how to draw a gradient in Swift and add an emoji on top. Anyone can be an "artist"!

# Using the cached assets

The server image feed intentionally returns some duplicate assets so you can play around with the scenario of getting an already-cached asset and displaying it.

When you look at Xcode's output console, you'll initially see some download logs like these:

```
Download: http://localhost:8080/gallery/image?11
Download: http://localhost:8080/gallery/image?16
Download: http://localhost:8080/gallery/image?23
Download: http://localhost:8080/gallery/image?26
```

Scroll all the way to the bottom of the feed, and you'll see that the download logs stop appearing in the console, even if you keep scrolling up and down. Once you've downloaded all the assets, you only fetch images from memory!

To wrap this section up, open **DetailsView.swift**, where you'll add some code to display a larger version of a selected asset.

Add the same `imageLoader` environment object property:

```
@EnvironmentObject var imageLoader: ImageLoader
```

Add a `task` modifier just below the existing `foregroundColor` modifier with the following code:

```
.task {
  image = try? await imageLoader.image(file.url)
}
```

Build and run. Tap an image and enjoy the details preview:

> **Note**: The details view shows the given unicode name for each emoji. Some of those names are pretty weird — I'm looking at you, "White Smiling Facevariation Selector16"!

Congratulations, the EmojiArt online catalog app is complete. Well, at least the part you had to work on in this chapter. You'll explore some more opportunities to use actors in the next chapter.

# Key points

- The **actor** type is a thread-safe type that protects its internals from concurrent access, supported by compile-time checks and diagnostics.

- Actors allow **"internal" synchronous access** to their state while the compiler enforces **asynchronous calls for access** from the "outside".

- Actor methods prefixed with the **nonisolated** keyword behave as standard class methods and provide no isolation mechanics.

- Actors use a runtime-managed **serial executor** to serialize calls to methods and access to properties.

- The **Sendable** protocol indicates a value is safe to use in a concurrent context. The **@Sendable** attribute requires a sendable value for a method or a closure parameter.

In this hands-on chapter, you designed both simple and complex actor-based code. Most importantly, you experienced some of the hurdles of converting unsafe class code to thread-safe actor code.

The fun isn't over yet, though. You'll keep working on the EmojiArt app as you learn about **global actors** in the next chapter.

For the grand finale, you'll once again search for alien life in Chapter 10, "Actors in a Distributed System", where you'll learn about using actors that work together across different devices.

# Chapter 9: Global Actors

By Marin Todorov

In the previous chapter, you got to meet Swift's actor type, which provides code with safe, concurrent access to its internal state. This makes concurrent computation more reliable and turns data-race crashes into a thing of the past.

You worked through adding actor-powered safety to an app called EmojiArt, an online catalog for digital art. Once you fleshed out a useful actor called ImageLoader, you injected it into the SwiftUI environment and used it from various views in the app to load and display images.

Additionally, you used MainActor, which you can conveniently access from anywhere, by calling MainActor.run(...). That's pretty handy given how often you need to make quick changes that drive the UI:

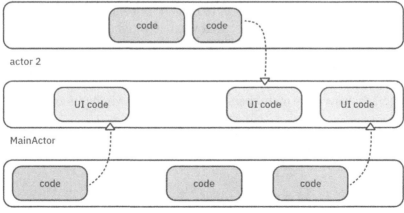

When you think about it, this is super-duper convenient: Because your app runs on a **single main thread**, you can't create a second or a third `MainActor`. So *it does* make sense that there's a default, shared instance of that actor that you can safely use from anywhere.

Some examples of app-wide, single-instance shared state are:

- The app's database layer, which is usually a singleton type that manages the state of a file on disk.

- Image or data caches are also often single-instance types.

- The authentication status of the user is valid app-wide, whether they have logged in or not.

Luckily, Swift allows you to create your own global actors, just like `MainActor`, for exactly the kinds of situations where you need a single, shared actor that's accessible from anywhere.

# Getting to meet GlobalActor

In Swift, you can annotate an actor with the `@globalActor` attribute, which makes it automatically conform to the `GlobalActor` protocol:

```
@globalActor actor myActor {
  ...
}
```

`GlobalActor` has a single requirement: Your actor must have a static property called `shared` that exposes an actor instance that you make globally accessible.

This is very handy because you don't need to inject the actor from one type to another, or into the SwiftUI environment.

Global actors, however, are more than just a stand-in for singleton types.

Just as you annotated methods with `@MainActor` to allow their code to change the app's UI, you can use the @-prefixed annotation to **automatically execute methods** on your own, custom global actor:

```
@MyActor func say(_ text: String) {
  ... automatically runs on MyActor ...
}
```

To automatically execute a method on your own global actor, annotate it with the name of your actor prefixed with an @ sign, like so: @MyActor, @DatabaseActor, @ImageLoader and so on.

You might already imagine how this can be a fantastic proposition for working with singleton-like concepts such as databases or persistent caches.

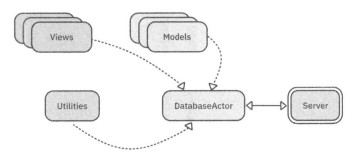

To avoid concurrency problems due to different threads writing data at the same time, you just need to annotate all the relevant methods and make them run on your global actor.

By using the @ annotation, you can **group** methods or entire types that can safely share mutable state in their own **synchronized silo**:

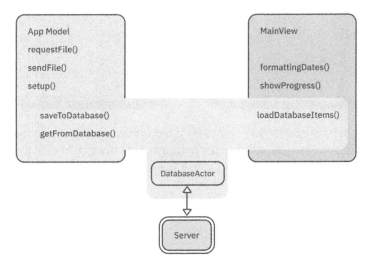

In this chapter, you'll add a persistent cache layer to the EmojiArt project that you worked on in the last chapter, as shown in the diagram above.

You'll get plenty of opportunities to learn about global actors in detail while having fun with juggling on-disk and in-memory caches.

# Continuing with the EmojiArt project

In this section, you'll keep working on the last chapter's project: **EmojiArt**, your online store for verified, digital emoji art:

In Chapter 8, "Getting Started With Actors", you implemented an actor-based, in-memory cache. Your `ImageLoader` actor manages a dictionary of completed downloads, failed downloads and those still being processed, so you don't fire duplicate requests to the server.

However, when you quit the app and run it again, it needs to fetch the images from the server all over again. They don't persist on the device.

This is a perfect opportunity for you to add a global actor to upgrade your app with a persistent, on-disk cache.

If you worked through the entirety of Chapter 8, "Getting Started With Actors", you can continue working on your own project. Otherwise, open the EmojiArt starter project in this chapter's materials from the **projects/starter** folder.

Before getting started with the project, start the book server. If you haven't already done that, navigate to the server folder **00-book-server** in the book materials-repository and enter `swift run`. The detailed steps are covered in Chapter 1, "Why Modern Swift Concurrency?".

At this point, you're all set to start working!

# Creating a global actor

In this section, you'll enhance EmojiArt with a new global actor that will persist downloaded images on disk.

To start, create a new Swift file and name it **ImageDatabase.swift**. Replace the placeholder code with the actor's bare bones:

```
import UIKit

@globalActor actor ImageDatabase {
    static let shared = ImageDatabase()

}
```

Here, you declare a new actor called `ImageDatabase` and annotate it with `@globalActor`. This makes the type conform to the `GlobalActor` protocol, which you satisfy by adding the `shared` property right away.

In more complex use cases, the shared instance could also be an actor of a different type. In this chapter, you'll use `shared` simply to facilitate access to the default instance of `ImageDatabase`.

Now, you can access your new actor type from anywhere by referring to the shared instance `ImageDatabase.shared`. Additionally, you can move the execution methods of other types to the `ImageDatabase` serial executor by annotating them with `@ImageDatabase`.

> **Note**: The `Actor` and `GlobalActor` protocols don't require an initializer. If you'd like to create new instances of your global actor, however, you can add a public or internal initializer. This is a valid approach when, for example, you create a custom instance to use in your unit tests.
>
> On the other hand, if you want to explicitly avoid creating other copies, add an `init()` and make it `private`.

To wrap up the basic actor structure and its state, add these properties to it:

```
let imageLoader = ImageLoader()

private let storage = DiskStorage()
private var storedImagesIndex: [String] = []
```

Now, your new actor will use an instance of `ImageLoader` to automatically fetch images that aren't already fetched from the server.

You also instantiate a class called `DiskStorage`, which handles the disk-access layer for you, so you don't have to write non-actor-related code. `DiskStorage` features simple file operation methods like reading, writing and deleting files from the app's caches.

Finally, you'll keep an index of the persisted files on disk in `storedImagesIndex`. This lets you avoid checking the file system every time you send a request to `ImageDatabase`.

Is it possible that you introduced some concurrency issues into your code with these few simple lines? You'll check that out next.

# Creating a safe silo

Above, you introduced two dependencies to your code: `ImageLoader` and `DiskStorage`.

You can be certain that `ImageLoader` doesn't introduce any concurrency issues, since it's an actor. But what about `DiskStorage`? Could that type lead to concurrency issues in your global actor?

You could argue that `storage` belongs to `ImageDatabase`, which is an actor. Therefore, `storage`'s code executes serially, and the code in `DiskStorage` cannot introduce data races.

That's a valid argument, but other threads, actors or functions can create their own instances of `DiskStorage`. In that case, the code **could be unreliable**.

One way to address this is to convert `DiskStorage` to an actor as well. However, since you mostly expect `ImageDatabase` to work with `DiskStorage`, making it an actor will introduce some redundant switching between actors.

What you really need, in this chapter, is to guarantee that the code in DiskStorage always runs on ImageDatabase's serial executor. This will eliminate concurrency issues and avoid excessive **actor hopping**.

ImageDatabase executor

To do this, open **DiskStorage.swift** and prepend the class declaration with @ImageDatabase, like this:

```
@ImageDatabase class DiskStorage {
```

Instead of DiskStorage's individual methods, you move the whole type to the ImageDatabase serial executor. This way, ImageDatabase and DiskStorage can never step on each other's toes.

That wasn't difficult at all, but you now face an error:

```
Call to global actor 'ImageDatabase'-isolated initializer
'init()' in a synchronous actor-isolated context
```

The Swift compiler's complaint is valid. You cannot create DiskStorage, which runs on ImageDatabase's serial executor, *before* you've created ImageDatabase itself.

You'll fix that by deferring the storage initialization to a new method called setUp(), along with a few other things you need to take care of when you initialize your database.

## Initializing the database actor

First, switch back to **ImageDatabase.swift**. Then, replace:

```
private let storage = DiskStorage()
```

With:

```
private var storage: DiskStorage!
```

Next, you'll add `setUp()`. Add the new method anywhere inside `ImageDatabase`:

```
func setUp() async throws {
  storage = await DiskStorage()
  for fileURL in try await storage.persistedFiles() {
    storedImagesIndex.append(fileURL.lastPathComponent)
  }
}
```

`setUp()` initializes `DiskStorage` and reads all the files persisted on disk into the `storedImagesIndex` lookup index. Any time you save new files to disk, you'll also update the index.

You'll need to ensure you call it before any other method in `ImageDatabase`, because you'll initialize your storage there. Don't worry about this for now, though. You'll take care of it in a moment.

## Writing files to disk

The new cache will need to write images to disk. When you fetch an image, you'll export it to PNG format and save it. To do that, add the following method anywhere inside `ImageDatabase`:

```
func store(image: UIImage, forKey key: String) async throws {
  guard let data = image.pngData() else {
    throw "Could not save image \(key)"
  }
  let fileName = DiskStorage.fileName(for: key)
  try await storage.write(data, name: fileName)
  storedImagesIndex.append(fileName)
}
```

Here, you get the image's PNG data and save it by using the `write(_:name:)` storage method. If that goes through successfully, you add the asset to the lookup index, too.

You now face a new compiler error. To fix it, open **DiskStorage.swift** and scroll to `fileName(for:)`.

Give the method a close inspection. It looks like this is a pure function that uses no state at all, so you can safely make it **non-isolated**, as you did for similar methods in the last chapter.

Prepend `nonisolated` to the method definition, like this:

```
nonisolated static func fileName(for path: String) -> String {
```

This clears the error and lets you move on.

# Fetching images from disk (or elsewhere)

Next, you'll add a helper method to fetch an image from the database. If the file is already stored on disk, you'll fetch it from there. Otherwise, you'll use `ImageLoader` to make a request to the server. This is how the completed flow will look:

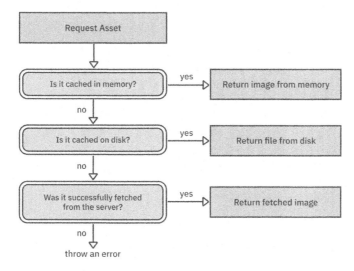

To implement this, add the initial code of the new method to `ImageDatabase`:

```
func image(_ key: String) async throws -> UIImage {
  if await imageLoader.cache.keys.contains(key) {
    print("Cached in-memory")
    return try await imageLoader.image(key)
  }

}
```

This method takes a path to an asset and either returns an image or throws an error.

Before trying the disk or the network, you check if you find a cached image in memory; if so, you can get it directly from ImageLoader.cache.

Because your caching strategy is getting more complex, you also add a new log message that lets you know you've successfully retrieved an in-memory image.

In case there's no cached asset in memory, you check the on-disk index and, if there's a match, you read the file and return it.

You'll now add the rest of the logic for querying the local image database for a cached asset, as well as falling back to fetching from the remote server if one doesn't exist.

Append the following to the same method:

```swift
do {
  // 1
  let fileName = DiskStorage.fileName(for: key)
  if !storedImagesIndex.contains(fileName) {
    throw "Image not persisted"
  }

  // 2
  let data = try await storage.read(name: fileName)
  guard let image = UIImage(data: data) else {
    throw "Invalid image data"
  }

  print("Cached on disk")
  // 3
  await imageLoader.add(image, forKey: key)
  return image
} catch {
  // 4
}
```

This block of code is a little longer, so look at it step-by-step:

1. You get the asset file name from DiskStorage.fileName(for:) and check the database index for a match. If the key doesn't exist, you throw an error that transfers the execution to the catch statement. You'll try fetching the asset from the server there.

2. You then try reading the file from disk and initializing a UIImage with its contents. Again, if either of these steps fails, you throw and try to get the image from the server in the catch block.

3.  Finally, if you successfully retrieved the cached image, you store it in memory in
    ImageLoader. This prevents you from having to make the trip to the file system
    and back next time.

4.  In the empty catch block, you'll fetch the asset from the server.

To complete the method, insert this code inside catch:

```
let image = try await imageLoader.image(key)
try await store(image: image, forKey: key)
return image
```

This code will run if all other local attempts fail and you have to make a network call
to the server. You call ImageLoader.image(_:) to fetch the image and, before
returning, store it on disk for future use.

With that, the persistence layer is almost ready. To complete it, you'll add one final
method for debugging purposes, just as you did for the image loader.

# Purging the cache

To easily test the caching logic, you'll add one more method to ImageDatabase.
clear() will delete all the asset files on disk and empty the index. Add the following
anywhere in ImageDatabase:

```
func clear() async {
  for name in storedImagesIndex {
    try? await storage.remove(name: name)
  }
  storedImagesIndex.removeAll()
}
```

Here, you iterate over all the indexed files in storedImagesIndex and try to delete
the matching files on disk. Finally, you remove all values from the index as well.

The cache is ready; it's time to use it in EmojiArt.

# Wiring up the persistence layer

As noted earlier, before you do anything with the new database type, you need to set it up safely by calling ImageDatabase's setUp method. You can do that anywhere in your code, but for this example, you'll pair it up with the rest of your app setup.

Open **LoadingView.swift** and scroll to task(...).

The first thing you currently do in the app is to call model.loadImages() in that task modifier. Insert the following **before** the line that calls loadImages():

```
try await ImageDatabase.shared.setUp()
```

With that wrinkle out of the way, your next step is to replace all the current calls to ImageLoader with ImageDatabase, instead.

Once you do this, you'll always make requests to ImageDatabase, which serializes the access and transparently uses the image loader when an image isn't cached locally. There are, all in all, only two occurrences you need to replace.

First, open **ThumbImage.swift** and replace imageLoader.image(file.url) inside the task(...) modifier with:

```
ImageDatabase.shared.image(file.url)
```

That will check the in-memory cache, then the on-disk cache and then, if all else fails, the network.

The completed task code should now look like this:

```
.task {
  guard let image = try? await
    ImageDatabase.shared.image(file.url) else {
    overlay = "camera.metering.unknown"
    return
  }
  updateImage(image)
}
```

You can also delete the imageLoader property, since you're not using it anymore.

Secondly, open **DetailsView.swift** and replace imageLoader.image(file.url) with:

```
ImageDatabase.shared.image(file.url)
```

Delete `imageLoader` here, as well.

Build and run. Direct your attention to the output console; you'll see a healthy mix of network requests and assets cached in memory, like so:

```
Download: http://localhost:8080/gallery/image?26
Cached in-memory
Cached in-memory
Download: http://localhost:8080/gallery/image?2
Cached in-memory
Download: http://localhost:8080/gallery/image?9
Download: http://localhost:8080/gallery/image?22
...
```

Without losing sight of the output console, scroll all the way to the bottom of the image feed, then scroll back to the top. Once you've downloaded all the images, you'll only see memory hits like this:

```
Cached in-memory
Cached in-memory
Cached in-memory
Cached in-memory
Cached in-memory
Cached in-memory
Cached in-memory
```

So far, so good! This is exactly how your pair of star actors should behave.

Now, for the ultimate test: Stop the app and run it again. Don't scroll the feed just yet!

This time, the disk cache serves all the content without you having to fetch it from the network:

```
Cached on disk
Cached on disk
Download: http://localhost:8080/gallery/image?10
Cached on disk
Cached on disk
```

Every now and again, you'll see a network request go through; these are the assets that failed to download on the last run of the app. You retry fetching those because they're not persisted on disk.

Scroll down to the bottom and up again. You'll see that after loading all the assets from disk, the log again fills up with messages for memory-cached assets.

Congratulations, it seems like all the pieces of the jigsaw puzzle have come together to create a super-powerful image caching mechanism for your project.

No time to spend gloating, though; you have a few more tasks to complete before wrapping up.

# Adding a cache hit counter

In this section, you'll add code to activate the bottom bar in the feed screen to help you debug your caching mechanism. This is how the toolbar will look when you finish:

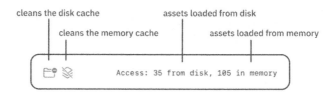

The toolbar consists of two buttons on the left side: one to clear the disk cache and one to clear the in-memory cache. On the right side, there's a cache hit counter that shows you how many assets you loaded from disk and how many from memory.

Right now, the toolbar doesn't do anything or show any real information. You'll work on it in this section.

First, you need to add a way for `ImageLoader` to continuously publish the count of cache hits. And, you guessed it, that sounds like a case for `AsyncStream`!

Open **ImageLoader.swift** and add these new properties:

```
@MainActor private(set) var inMemoryAccess: AsyncStream<Int>?

private var inMemoryAcccessContinuation:
AsyncStream<Int>.Continuation?
private var inMemoryAccessCounter = 0 {
  didSet
{ inMemoryAcccessContinuation?.yield(inMemoryAccessCounter) }
}
```

Here, you add a new asynchronous stream called `inMemoryAccess` that runs on the main actor. Your views can access and subscribe to this property without worrying about any background UI updates.

Additionally, you protect the current count in inMemoryAccessCounter, by leveraging ImageLoader's actor semantics. You'll store the stream continuation in inMemoryAcccessContinuation so you can easily produce ongoing updates. Finally, the didSet accessor ensures that any updates to inMemoryAccessCounter are relayed to the continuation, if one exists.

To correctly initialize the stream, you'll add setUp() to ImageLoader, as you previously did for your other actor. Insert the following anywhere inside the type:

```
func setUp() async {
  let accessStream = AsyncStream<Int> { continuation in
    inMemoryAcccessContinuation = continuation
  }
  await MainActor.run { inMemoryAccess = accessStream }
}
```

In setUp(), you create a new AsyncStream and store its continuation in inMemoryAcccessContinuation. Then, switching to the main actor, you store the stream itself in inMemoryAccess.

With this setup, you can produce new values at any given time by calling inMemoryAcccessContinuation.yield(...). To do that, scroll to image(_:) and find this case: case .completed(let image). Insert this code on the next line, before the return statement:

```
inMemoryAccessCounter += 1
```

Here, you increase the hit counter, which in return yields the result to the stored continuation. Since both properties are on the actor, you perform both operations synchronously. However, the @MainActor annotation causes the stream to produce the value on the main actor asynchronously:

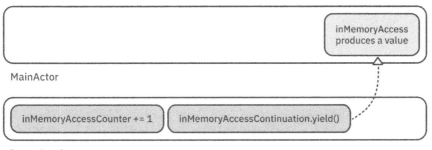

As a good developer, you'll also add a deinitializer to manually complete the stream when the actor is released from memory:

```
deinit {
  inMemoryAcccessContinuation?.finish()
}
```

# Displaying the counter

You'll get around to updating your view code in a moment, but don't forget that the image loader will not set itself up automatically. You'll now add the call to `ImageLoader.setUp()`, just like you did for `ImageDatabase`.

A safe place to call `ImageLoader.setUp()` is your database's own `setUp()`. Open **ImageDatabase.swift** and find `setUp()`. Append the following to the bottom of the method:

```
await imageLoader.setUp()
```

With that out of the way, you can move on to updating the UI code that displays the debugging toolbar at the bottom of the image feed.

Open **BottomToolbar.swift**; add a new `task` modifier after the last `padding` in the code:

```
.task {
  guard let memoryAccessSequence =
    ImageDatabase.shared.imageLoader.inMemoryAccess else {
    return
  }
  for await count in memoryAccessSequence {
    inMemoryAccessCount = count
  }
}
```

Above, you unwrap the optional stream and use a `for await` loop to asynchronously iterate over the sequence.

Each time the stream produces a value, you assign it to `inMemoryAccessCount` — a state property on the toolbar view that you use to display the text in the toolbar.

Build and run again. Scroll up and down a little, and you'll see the in-memory counter give you updates in real-time:

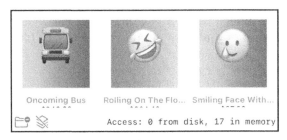

## Purging the in-memory cache

To complete the last exercise for this chapter, you'll wire up the button that clears the memory cache.

First, you'll add a new method to `ImageLoader` to purge the in-memory assets. Then, you'll wire up the toolbar button.

Open **ImageDatabase.swift** and add this new method that encapsulates clearing the image loader cache:

```
func clearInMemoryAssets() async {
  await imageLoader.clear()
}
```

Then switch back to **BottomToolbar.swift** and find the comment that reads `// Clear in-memory cache`.

This code is for the right button in the toolbar. Replace the comment with the actual code to clear the memory cache:

```
Task {
  await ImageDatabase.shared.clearInMemoryAssets()
  try await model.loadImages()
}
```

In the code above, you first clear the in-memory cache, then reload the images from the server.

Build and run. Tap the button to check that the app correctly clears the memory, then gets all the assets from the network once again.

Now that you've completed that last feature, the EmojiArt app is complete. You've done a fantastic job working through all the steps in this chapter.

Feel free to jump over to the next chapter if you're eager to move on to the next topic: **distributed actors**. If you'd like to work on EmojiArt a bit longer, stay for this chapter's challenge.

# Challenges:

## Challenge: Updating the number of disk fetches

In this challenge, you'll finish the debugging toolbar by connecting the second counter, which displays on-disk cache hits.

Your approach should be similar to what you did in the last section of the chapter for the in-memory counter; it shouldn't take you long.

In your implementation, follow these general steps, mirroring what you did for `ImageLoader`:

- Add an async stream for the counter to `ImageDatabase`.

- Set up the stream in the actor's `setUp()`.

- Complete the stream in a deinitializer.

- Increment the counter when you have an actual disk cache hit.

- Finally, update the toolbar view to iterate over the stream and make the last toolbar button clear the disk cache.

After you've finished working through these steps, the toolbar will be an excellent debugging tool to verify and test your caching logic:

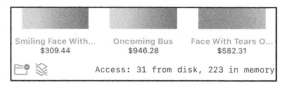

# Key points

- **Global actors** protect the global mutable state within your app.

- Use **@globalActor** to annotate an actor as global and make it conform to the GlobalActor protocol.

- Use a global actor's **serial executor** to form concurrency-safe silos out of code that needs to work with the same mutable state.

- Use a mix of **actors** and **global actors**, along with **async/await** and **asynchronous sequences**, to make your concurrent code safe.

By completing the EmojiArt project, you've gained a solid understanding of the problems that actors solve and how to use these fancy APIs to write solid and safe concurrent code.

However, there's still one kind of actor you haven't tried yet. **Distributed actors** are, in fact, *so bleeding-edge* that they're still a work in progress, and you'll have to partially implement them on your own. If that sounds like a cool challenge, turn the page to the next and final chapter of this book.

# Chapter 10: Actors in a Distributed System

By Marin Todorov

In the previous chapters, you learned how to run concurrent tasks in parallel on multiple CPU cores. Furthermore, you learned how to use actor types to make concurrency safe. In this last chapter of the book, you'll cover the advanced topic of **distributed actors**: actors that run not only locally, but also in other processes — or even on *different machines* altogether.

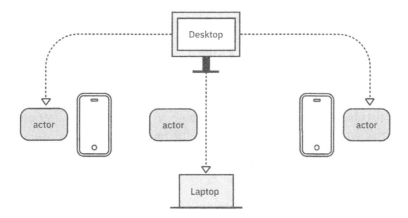

At the time of this writing, Apple is:

- Gathering feedback on an experimental distributed actors language feature through a Swift Evolution process pitch (https://forums.swift.org/t/pitch-distributed-actors/51669). Once the proposal is accepted, the feature will land in a future release of Swift.

- Working on and implementing feedback for a "Swift Distributed Actors (https://swift.org/blog/distributed-actors/)" package — a cluster library for the upcoming distributed actor language feature.

Since these are currently works-in-progress, you'll build your own **custom distributed system** in this chapter, to play around with the idea of using actors in a distributed environment. You'll only use local actors for now, and you'll write your own logic to make them cooperate across the network.

Once Apple merges the distributed actors language feature in an upcoming Swift release, we'll update this chapter to remove the custom implementation and redesign the step-by-step instructions to use the latest and greatest syntax.

> **Note**: The generic design of the language syntax for distributed actors is thoroughly described in the proposal linked above. In a few places in this chapter, we'll make a parallel between your custom implementation and how the feature is likely to work when it ships.

The distributed actors model has been around for some time, and libraries offer actors and distributed actors for many languages. Therefore, this chapter includes only a minimal amount of theory that covers the model in general, since Apple hasn't released that language feature just yet.

Without further ado — could distributed actors come to the stage, please?

# Going from local to distributed

You're already familiar with actors — they let you isolate state by putting an automatic barrier between the type's synchronized internal state and access from "outside" the synchronized scope. That means that calls from other types are considered **outside access** and automatically made asynchronous:

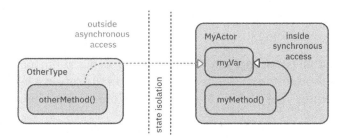

Since accessing the actor's state from outside is done asynchronously, that process may take an arbitrary amount of time. In fact, in Chapter 6, "Testing Asynchronous Code", you had to implement a custom way to time out asynchronous calls that took longer than expected.

For local actors, the compiler transparently serializes calls that access the actor's state:

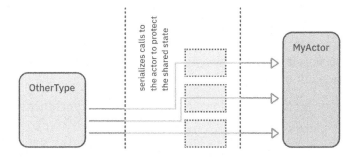

But the compiler isn't limited to always injecting the same logic into the isolation layer. For example, distributed actors take advantage of the isolation layer's asynchronous nature and allow you to add a **transport service** there. A transport can relay calls to actor methods to another process, to another machine on the network or to a JSON API available on a web server.

Distributed actors introduce the notion of location transparency, which allows you to work with both local and distributed actors in much the same way. In fact, at the point-of-use in your app, they're interchangeable with very few code changes. Furthermore, location transparency makes it easy to develop your actors locally and release them into a distributed environment. Or, vice versa, you can develop distributed actors and design their unit tests to run locally!

You can choose *any kind* of transport because the distributed actor language feature is **transport agnostic**! You can talk to an actor over the network, through Bluetooth connectivity or via custom JSON API of your choice.

For example, in a shopping app, you could call a userOrders() actor method to get a user's orders. A transport service forwards your call to the server, where an actor counterpart executes usersOrders() and reads the orders from the server database:

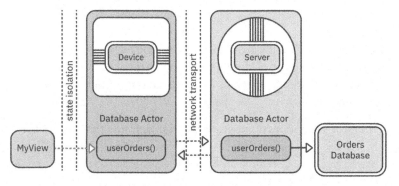

The diagram above shows an example of working with a local database actor that transparently forwards database queries to a server on the web. Your UI layer, MyView, doesn't know if the database actor is local or distributed — it doesn't make a difference at the point of use.

If that looks a little bit like magic, don't fret; distributed actors function by strict rules that make it all possible.

Distributed actors have the following traits:

- They allow **no direct access to data** from outside the actor. The model encourages async method calls, which are easy to relay over the transport layer.

- Distributed actors are **addressable**. Depending on the type of transport, a distributed actor's address may be a REST endpoint, a local process ID, a file path or something else that uniquely identifies it.

- The input and output of actor methods are automatically **serialized for transport**.

Once the distributed actors language feature ships, most of the traits above will be built in, letting you focus exclusively on designing your business logic. Until then, if you want to create your own distributed systems, you'll need to write a little more code — as you'll do in this chapter.

## Getting started with SkyNet

Once more, you'll work on the Sky project from Chapter 7, "Concurrent Code With TaskGroup". You'll improve it by adding an actor system that connects to local network devices over **Bonjour**. This will let you perform more concurrent scans by using system resources across the network.

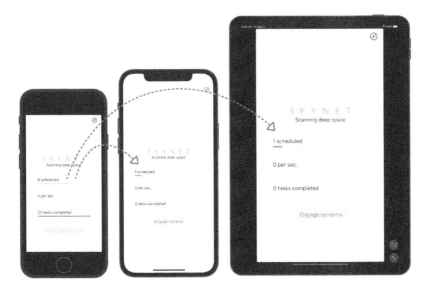

This chapter is fairly long. It features a lot of small steps that guide you through all parts of the project, like user interface, networking and concurrency. Should you feel a little fatigue coming over you, there's no shame in taking a break when you need it.

The ultimate goal for this guided exercise is to scale the computing power of the app by connecting more and more devices to a meshed Sky network. Thus, this chapter's project is called **SkyNet**.

Before you can add new features, you'll need to enable some useful code that's been hiding in the starter project.

## Enabling the network layer

At the end of Chapter 7, "Concurrent Code With TaskGroup", you left the Sky project — an app that scans satellite images for alien life signs — in good shape. The user can start a scan by tapping **Engage systems**, and the app will concurrently iterate over sectors in satellite imagery and scan them.

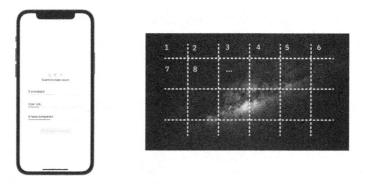

Open the starter project for this chapter — or, if you worked through Chapter 7, "Concurrent Code With TaskGroup" completely, you can continue working with your earlier project.

SkyNet will use **Bonjour** to discover other iOS devices running the app and talk to them. Bonjour (https://apple.co/2Xiax0Y) is a standard that Apple created to help your network discover devices and services.

For example, Bonjour lets you automatically find all the printers on the office Wi-Fi, letting you choose which one to use to print your resume. Which you'll need to do, now that you've updated it with all your new concurrency knowledge!

Even basic networking requires a lot of boilerplate. To save some time and help you focus on this chapter's main topic, the starter project already includes the bare bones of a functioning transport service over Bonjour.

Open **ScanTransport.swift** from the **Transport** folder and **uncomment** all the code that's commented. You'll find the opening comment syntax /* just below the copyright message and module imports at the top of the file and the closing */ at the very bottom. Remove them both.

You'll get two compiler errors, but don't worry — you'll fix those next.

In summary, `ScanTransport` creates a Bonjour network session, starts an advertiser service that tells other devices about the current system and starts a browser that finds other systems on the network:

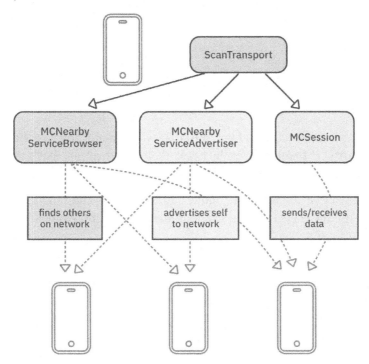

The bundled code connects all the SkyNet devices to one other and uses `NotificationCenter` to broadcast connection updates within your app.

You'll work on `ScanTransport` a little later, once you're ready to talk to other devices. For now, you need to create the missing `ScanSystem` type that the compiler is complaining about.

# Creating an actor system

In this section, you'll add an **actor system** to the project — a system that controls how scan tasks execute on a single machine. The app model will execute tasks via the local system. By the end of the chapter, it will detect other devices on the network and use their systems, too.

You'll start by creating a scanning system that will manage running tasks locally and remotely. Add a new file to the **Tasks** folder and call it **ScanSystem.swift**. Then, add the following actor code inside it:

```swift
import Foundation

actor ScanSystem {
  let name: String
  let service: ScanTransport?

  init(name: String, service: ScanTransport? = nil) {
    self.name = name
    self.service = service
  }
}
```

ScanSystem is a simple actor that you initialize with a name and a service. The service will transport the data over the network. In other words, that's the type that will relay tasks to remote systems.

The systems in SkyNet each need a unique address so they can send task requests to one another. You'll use each device's vendor identifier to anonymously identify the device on your local network.

Next, insert this code inside ScanSystem:

```swift
private(set) var count = 0

func commit() {
  count += 1
}

func run(_ task: ScanTask) async throws -> String {
  defer { count -= 1 }
  return try await task.run()
}
```

Here, you add:

- A thread-safe `count` property to track the current system's pending tasks.

- `commit()`, which increases the task counter. The system commits to performing the scan — that is, it's already accounting for the task — but waits for you to start the actual work by calling `run(_:)`. This design gives you a little more flexibility when distributing the work across systems.

- `run(_:)`, which runs the given task and decreases the `count` counter. The counter is safe to update even in concurrent calls because `ScanSystem` is an actor.

You'll work more on this actor later in the chapter. For now, leave it as it is and move on to updating the app model.

# Connecting to remote systems

To stay in touch with other systems on the network, you'll need to keep a list of their addresses. `ScanTransport` already takes care of connecting all the nodes, but it's up to you to do the "talking" between them.

To manage the list of connected SkyNet devices, you'll add one more actor. Add a new Swift file to the **Tasks** folder and name it **Systems.swift**.

Next, add the skeleton for the new type:

```swift
import Foundation

actor Systems {
  private(set) var systems: [ScanSystem]

  init(_ localSystem: ScanSystem) {
    systems = [localSystem]
  }
}
```

The new actor will manage a list of `ScanSystems`, one for each device connected to SkyNet.

The actor always starts with a single system on its list: the local one. To make it easily accessible, add a new computed property:

```swift
var localSystem: ScanSystem { systems[0] }
```

Next, you need a safe way to add and remove systems. Add these two convenience methods to do that:

```
func addSystem(name: String, service: ScanTransport) {
  removeSystem(name: name)
  let newSystem = ScanSystem(name: name, service: service)
  systems.append(newSystem)
}

func removeSystem(name: String) {
  systems.removeAll { $0.name == name }
}
```

Here's a breakdown of the code above:

- **addSystem(name:service:)**: Adds a new system. It also removes duplicate systems with the same name, if such systems exist.

- **removeSystem(name:)**: Removes any systems with the given name from the list.

Now that you've more or less completed the Systems type, you'll continue working in the app model. There, you'll watch out for connectivity messages and keep track of your connected SkyNet peers.

# Monitoring your systems' connectivity

Open **ScanModel.swift** and add these new properties:

```
@MainActor @Published var isConnected = false
private var systems: Systems
private(set) var service: ScanTransport
```

You have some big plans for those properties, namely:

- You'll update isConnected every time a system joins or leaves SkyNet, so you can update the app UI accordingly.

- systems is your systems actor. It manages the list of connected devices.

- You'll store the transport service in service and inject it into any remote systems, so they can use it to talk to other devices.

Each device will keep a list of all addresses so it can send requests to any of them.

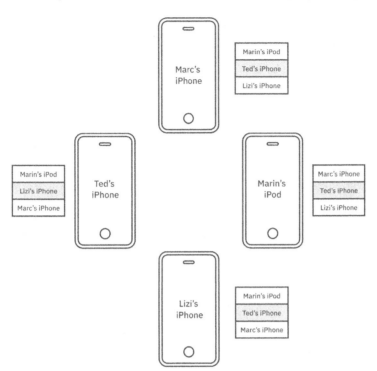

To resolve the errors regarding uninitialized properties, add these lines to the model's `init(total:localName:)` initializer:

```
let localSystem = ScanSystem(name: localName)
systems = Systems(localSystem)
service = ScanTransport(localSystem: localSystem)
service.taskModel = self
```

Here, you create a new system with the local device name and initialize your system's actor and the network transport.

Open **ScanTransport.swift** and scroll to `session(_:peer:didChange)`. This is an `MCSessionDelegate` that the **Multipeer Connectivity session**, `MCSession`, calls whenever a peer's connectivity changes.

`ScanTransport` is mostly interested in devices connecting or disconnecting; the code inside the method reacts only to `connected` and `disconnected` events and republishes those via `NotificationCenter`.

It also attaches the concrete peer device identifier to each notification. This is the identifier you'll use as the address of the respective remote system.

With that information in mind, switch back to **ScanModel.swift** and implement the system connectivity handler. Add this empty method to get started:

```
func systemConnectivityHandler() {
  Task {

  }
  Task {

  }
}
```

You'll use two asynchronous tasks to listen for the two notifications.

Start by adding this code inside the first Task closure:

```
for await notification in
  NotificationCenter.default.notifications(named: .connected) {

  guard let name = notification.object as? String else
{ continue }
  print("[Notification] Connected: \(name)")
  await systems.addSystem(name: name, service: self.service)
  Task { @MainActor in
    isConnected = await systems.systems.count > 1
  }
}
```

As in previous chapters, you asynchronously iterate over the notifications with a given name — in this case, connected. Each time you get a notification, you add a remote system with the connected peer identifier, too.

You need to update isConnected on the main actor; usually, you'd use MainActor.run(...) to do that. This time, however, you need to use await to access systems.count asynchronously — but MainActor.run(...) expects a synchronous closure.

So, instead of calling MainActor, you create a new Task and annotate the closure argument with @MainActor. This allows you to comfortably both use await in a concurrent context and run the code on the main actor.

Next, add this code inside the second task closure:

```
for await notification in
  NotificationCenter.default.notifications(named: .disconnected)
{

  guard let name = notification.object as? String else
{ return }
  print("[Notification] Disconnected: \(name)")
  await systems.removeSystem(name: name)
  Task { @MainActor in
    isConnected = await systems.systems.count > 1
  }
}
```

This task is similar to the previous one. Here, you remove a system by its name if the peer has disconnected.

All that's left is to call the new method. To do that, append this line to init(total:localName:):

```
systemConnectivityHandler()
```

You've now finished handling the systems in your model, from creating a local system and starting the discovery service to updating the list of connected peers.

Next, to make connecting a little more fun, you'll add an indicator to notify the user when their device is connected to SkyNet.

# Adding a connectivity indicator

Open **SkyApp.swift** and, just below the alert view modifier, insert:

```
.toolbar {
  if scanModel.isConnected {
    Image(systemName: "link.circle")
  }
}
```

With this code, whenever your model connects to one or more remote systems and updates isConnected, you'll show or hide the connection icon in the toolbar, too.

You've done a great job powering through this long list of steps. Now, it's finally time to try the new stuff!

Build and run.

There's a good chance that the first thing you'll notice is a macOS system alert that asks you if **Sky.app** is allowed to talk to other devices over the local network:

If you see this dialog, click **Allow** to give SkyNet access to the network; that will take you to the app's main screen:

**Note**: If you're running on a device, you might see the alert on your device instead.

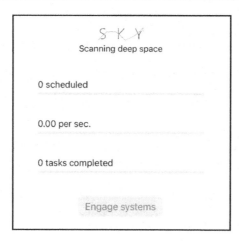

You don't see much difference from how the app looked at the end of Chapter 7, "Concurrent Code With TaskGroup", do you?

Of course not — at this point, SkyNet is only running on a *single* device. This is *not* SkyNet — it's just the Sky project. Tap the **Engage systems** button; you'll see that the app works just as it did before.

Luckily, Xcode allows you to start multiple iOS simulators at the same time! While you're running the project, select a different simulator from the device list next to the scheme selector:

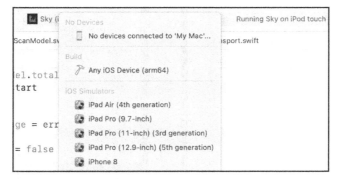

Once you start the app on a second or a third simulator, Xcode will stop the app on the previously running simulator. You'll need to manually restart SkyNet on the simulator(s) where the app has been stopped so you can have a few copies of the app working together.

> **Note**: If you have an older Mac, it might not be happy running multiple simulators at the same time, and it might not be able to devote multiple cores to multiple simulators. In that case, you'll need to run at least one copy of the app on a device to see the best results.

As soon as you launch the project on your additional device, you'll see the connectivity icon appear in the top-right corner:

Note that the connectivity framework is quite verbose. The output console fills up quickly with messages along the lines of:

```
[MCNearbyDiscoveryPeerConnection] Read failed.
[MCNearbyDiscoveryPeerConnection] Stream error occurred: Code=54
"Connection reset by peer"
[Notification] Connected: iPhone 12
[GCKSession] Failed to send a DTLS packet with 117 bytes;
sendmsg error: No route to host (65).
[GCKSession] Something is terribly wrong; no clist for remoteID
[1104778395] channelID [-1].
...
```

For the most part, you can ignore these messages. They make looking for your own logs a little difficult, but the connectivity framework usually quiets down after a few moments.

Congratulations, you're halfway there! Your actors are all on stage; now you have to give them some lines and direction. Your next task is to make those remote systems listen to your commands and jump hoops when you tell them to.

# Sending a task to a remote system

Next, you want to send a ScanTask over the network for remote execution. To do this, you need to make it Codable. Open **ScanTask.swift** and add a Codable conformance to that type:

```
struct ScanTask: Identifiable, Codable {
```

Now, open **ScanTransport.swift** and add this new method to ScanTransport:

```
func send(
  task: ScanTask,
  to recipient: String
) async throws -> String {
  guard let targetPeer = session.connectedPeers.first(
    where: { $0.displayName == recipient }) else {
      throw "Peer '\(recipient)' not connected anymore."
    }

  let payload = try JSONEncoder().encode(task)
  try session.send(payload, toPeers: [targetPeer],
with: .reliable)
}
```

Right off the bat, you'll notice a new compiler error, complaining that you haven't returned a value. Don't worry about it; you'll fix it momentarily.

The method accepts a task and a remote system name to talk to. First, you verify that the current system list contains the given identifier. In a real-life situation, the given system could have disconnected moments earlier, so you need to double-check.

Then, you send the encoded JSON payload by calling MCSession.send(...). You've already found the peer ID, so you ask the session to send the task payload to only that particular device.

Unfortunately, MCSession is not a modern type that offers async variants of their APIs. Since you can't comfortably await the remote peer response, you'll have to code that logic yourself.

# Managing a network request lifetime

There are three possible outcomes of sending a network request to another SkyNet system:

1.  ScanTransport receives a response from the remote peer with the task result. You'll add some code later to broadcast a response notification with the response payload.

2.  No response comes back within a given amount of time. You'll consider the peer **unresponsive** and abort the remote task execution.

3.  The remote peer disconnects while you're waiting for a response from it. In that case, you'll also fail the remote task execution.

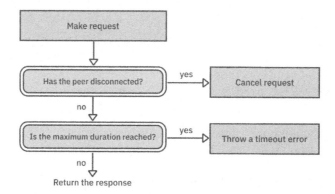

In a real app, there could be even more reasons for the remote task to fail, but you'll also have more time to develop and test the project. For this chapter, you'll implement the three options above.

You'll take care of the request timeout first of all. To do so, you'll use an old friend: TimeoutTask, which you used in Chapter 6, "Testing Asynchronous Code". Your current project includes TimeoutTask in the same state as at the end of that chapter.

Open **TimeoutTask.swift** in the **Utility** project folder. With your new knowledge about state isolation in Swift, it's fairly obvious that the code in TimeoutTask is crash-prone. If your code uses or updates continuation concurrently, it might **crash your app**. You noted that shortcoming of TimeoutTask when you first wrote the code; now, you'll finally resolve that issue.

In this chapter, you'll use the fact that actors serialize access to their state to easily prevent app crashes in SkyNet. Replace the `class` keyword near the top of the file with `actor`, like so:

```
actor TimeoutTask<Success> {
```

This simple change makes sure you won't cause any crashes that will bring down SkyNet because the `actor` type serializes the access to `continuation` as an instance property.

To use your newly minted actor, switch back to **ScanTransport.swift**. Find `send(task:to:)` and append the following at the bottom of it:

```
let networkRequest = TimeoutTask(seconds: 5) { () -> String in

}
```

Here, you create a new task that will time out if it doesn't get a response from the remote peer within five seconds. `TimeoutTask`'s result is the string that you expect the remote peer to return after completing the scan.

The code you'll add in the next section will accept peer responses and relay them to your model via notifications. Then, you'll wait for a `response` notification and return the remote result of the `TimeoutTask`.

# Receiving a response from a remote system

At this point, you need to add a new type that can transport the result of a scan *back* to the original system. You need a simple type to wrap the string that `Task.run()` returns.

> **Note:** The data you transport over the network isn't limited to a specific type. For simplicity's sake, you use a `String` here because encoding data for transport will become automatic anyway, once Apple merges its distributed actors support to Swift.

Open **ScanTask.swift** and add the following response type at the bottom of that file:

```
struct TaskResponse: Codable {
  let result: String
  let id: UUID
}
```

Now, switch back to **ScanTransport.swift** and return to send(task:to:). Inside TimeoutTask's closure, insert this code to handle response notifications:

```
for await notification in
  NotificationCenter.default.notifications(named: .response) {

  guard let response = notification.object as? TaskResponse,
        response.id == task.id else { continue }
  return "\(response.result) by \(recipient)"
}
fatalError("Will never execute")
```

The play-by-play here is:

- You asynchronously iterate over the notification center's sequence of .response notifications.

- If the response has an associated TaskResponse and its ID matches your request ID, it's the response you've been waiting for!

- Finally, to make the compiler happy, you add a fatalError() to clear the missing return statement error at the end of the closure.

No worries, your execution will never get to that fatal error. You'll either return a response match or the task will time out and throw a TimeoutError.

To take care of the third and final scenario from your list, add one more asynchronous task at the end of the method. It will run concurrently with the one that waits for a response:

```
Task {
  for await notification in

NotificationCenter.default.notifications(named: .disconnected) {

    guard notification.object as? String == recipient else
{ continue }
    await networkRequest.cancel()
  }
}
```

In a similar fashion as before, you asynchronously observe a `disconnected` notification. If you're waiting for a response from a peer that **disconnects**, you simply cancel the request altogether.

You've almost finished with *this* method; the only remaining step is to make `send(task:to:)` wait for `networkRequest`'s result and return it. To do that, append a `return` statement:

```
return try await networkRequest.value
```

The code you've added above will finally clear the compiler errors. Now, you can continue with the rest of the supporting methods that handle the back-and-forth communication between SkyNet peers.

# Executing requests from other systems

In this section, you'll add a method to your model that executes a task when a remote system asks it to do so. In the end, there's no point in asking remote systems to run tasks if they don't really do it, right?

Open **ScanModel.swift** and add this new method anywhere inside `ScanModel`:

```
func run(_ task: ScanTask) async throws -> String {
  Task { @MainActor in scheduled += 1 }
  defer {
    Task { @MainActor in scheduled -= 1 }
  }
  return try await systems.localSystem.run(task)
}
```

In this method, you accept a `ScanTask` and execute it on the local system while properly updating the task counter.

Unlike the code in `runAllTasks()`, the newly added `run(_:)` method always uses the local system and only updates the `scheduled` model property. `run(_:)` lets you run remotely created tasks and still update the Scheduled indicator to show the user that the device is working, even if they didn't tap **Engage systems** themselves.

# Sending a result back

You've made a lot of progress in this chapter! You've now reached the point when you'll send the result of a scan back to the original system.

In **ScanTransport.swift**, add this new method to `ScanTransport`:

```swift
func send(response: TaskResponse, to peerID: MCPeerID) throws {
  guard session.connectedPeers.contains(peerID) else {
    throw "Peer '\(peerID)' not connected anymore."
  }

  let payload = try JSONEncoder().encode(response)
  try session.send(payload, toPeers: [peerID], with: .reliable)
}
```

Sending a response is relatively straightforward compared to sending the request — you just send it off and don't need to wait for a response back from the original peer.

Just as in `send(task:to:)`, you verify that the target peer is in the list of connected devices; if so, you use the connectivity session to send the encoded payload.

# Handling incoming data

With the methods to send requests and responses in place, you also need to add the session handler method that accepts data and handles it correctly, depending on whether it's an incoming request or a response.

In `ScanTransport`, scroll to the `session(_:didReceive:fromPeer:)` placeholder. `MCSession` calls that delegate method when a peer on the network sends data to the device. You'll add your dispatcher code here.

Start by adding a decoder:

```swift
let decoder = JSONDecoder()
```

You'll use `decoder` throughout the method to decode the incoming data.

First, check if the incoming data is a `ScanTask`. Add:

```swift
if let task = try? decoder.decode(ScanTask.self, from: data) {

}
```

If you successfully decode the data as a ScanTask, that means another SkyNet node is asking you to run the task locally. As a good peer, you'll do it. Insert this task inside the if statement:

```
Task { [weak self] in
  guard let self = self,
        let taskModel = self.taskModel else { return }

  let result = try await taskModel.run(task)
  let response = TaskResponse(result: result, id: task.id)
  try self.send(response: response, to: peerID)
}
```

In this asynchronous task, you:

• Unwrap the model object from the weakly captured self.

• Run the task on the model — and, in turn, on the local system.

• Create a TaskResponse value with the task result and the original task ID.

• Call your newly minted method to send responses.

It's nice to see the pieces of the jigsaw puzzle fit together so neatly!

Next, don't lose your inertia — quickly move on to handling the responses.

## Handling responses

Append the following to the bottom of session(_:didReceive:fromPeer:):

```
if let response = try? decoder
  .decode(TaskResponse.self, from: data) {

  NotificationCenter.default.post(
    name: .response,
    object: response
  )
}
```

If you can decode the data as a TaskResponse, it means you've asked a remote system to run an errand for you, and it's sending the result.

In this case, you have another ongoing task waiting for that response in `send(task:to:)`. To complete the data flow back to that method, you send a response notification that the `for` loop in `send(task:to:)`'s `TimeoutTask` will handle.

If the data is neither a request nor a response, you'll ignore it and let the method return without doing anything.

# Putting everything together

To review, you've taken care of the following issues so far:

- Creating a system to run tasks.

- Connecting remote systems over SkyNet.

- Sending tasks for remote execution.

- Sending results back to the origin system.

The last missing piece is to alter your model to use these new features.

Neat as it is, the current approach to running a limited amount of tasks via `TaskGroup` won't handle the logic of spreading the work over multiple systems.

Before you replace the code in `runAllTasks()`, you need a new helper method on your `Systems` actor to allow you to find the first system in the list that is available to run the next task.

Open **Systems.swift** and add a new actor method:

```
func firstAvailableSystem() async -> ScanSystem {
  while true {
    for nextSystem in systems where await nextSystem.count < 4 {
      await nextSystem.commit()
      return nextSystem
    }
    await Task.sleep(seconds: 0.1)
  }
  fatalError("Will never execute")
}
```

`firstAvailableSystem()` uses the `count` property on `ScanSystem` to search for a system that isn't overloaded with work and can run new tasks.

You always start by checking the first element in `systems`, so you'll use up all the capacity on the local system before trying to send tasks over the network.

If there aren't any systems with free capacity available, you wait briefly, then check the list — again and again — until a system frees up and is ready for more work.

As you did earlier, you added a `fatalError` to satisfy the compiler's hunger for a `return` statement at the end, even if the execution will never get to that line.

You're finally ready to replace `runAllTasks()`' implementation. Back in **ScanModel.swift**, replace `runAllTasks()` with a clean starter version:

```
func runAllTasks() async throws {
  started = Date()
  try await withThrowingTaskGroup(
    of: Result<String, Error>.self
  ) { [unowned self] group in

    for try await result in group {
      switch result {
      case .success(let result):
        print("Completed: \(result)")
      case .failure(let error):
        print("Failed: \(error.localizedDescription)")
      }
    }
    await MainActor.run {
      completed = 0
      countPerSecond = 0
      scheduled = 0
    }
    print("Done.")
  }
}
```

This is mostly made up of the existing code, but it excludes the lines that add tasks to the group. You reset the `started` property to clock the scan duration at completion. You then start a throwing group that contains the code to loop over the group tasks and print the results. Finally, you reset the model counters.

The "missing" part in the task group is the code to actually run the tasks — you'll add this in again in a moment.

Before you finalize the new implementation, you need to update `worker(number:)`, which is the method that actually runs the scans.

Scroll to `worker(number:)` in the same file and update its definition to:

```
func worker(number: Int, system: ScanSystem) async
  -> Result<String, Error> {
```

Then, inside the method body replace the `result = try await task.run()` line with:

```
result = try await system.run(task)
```

These two changes will pipe the task execution through to the given system instead of always running it locally.

This is a good time to make sure your tasks run locally or remotely, as needed, depending on the execution context.

Open **ScanSystem.swift** and replace `return try await task.run()` in `run(_:)` with:

```
if let service = service {
  return try await service.send(task: task, to: name)
} else {
  return try await task.run()
}
```

Just as planned, if the system is remote, you send the task through the transport service. Otherwise, you execute the task locally.

Now, it's time to go back to **ScanModel.swift** and complete the changes in `runAllTasks()`. Append this code before the existing `for` loop:

```
for number in 0 ..< total {
  let system = await systems.firstAvailableSystem()
  group.addTask {
    return await self.worker(number: number, system: system)
  }
}
```

Before scheduling each task, you fetch the first available system. If there's no free capacity, you might need to wait a while; but ultimately, this code will return an available system. Effectively, you've outsourced the logic to limit the number of concurrent scans per system to `firstAvailableSystem()`.

Inside each task, you call `worker(number:system:)` and return its result.

To quickly verify your code changes, build and run. The app will behave similarly to how it did before. Tap **Engage Systems** and you'll notice a max of four tasks are scheduled on the local devices, as defined by your resource distribution logic above:

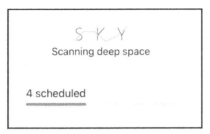

You'll add one more cool feature before trying out SkyNet on multiple devices.

# Adding some UI bling

While it's pretty impressive to make simulators join SkyNet and work together, presentation is important, too. Right now, collaborating on the search for alien life seems a little... *unspectacular.*

Before moving onto the last few heavy-duty tasks in this chapter, you'll include a little animation that you'll display onscreen when devices connect and start a joint scan session. Since the starter project includes the animation already, you just need to set the `ScanModel.isCollaborating` flag to `true` when you're performing joint work.

To update `isCollaborating` at the right time, add this `didSet` handler to the `scheduled` property in `ScanModel`, so it looks like this:

```
@MainActor @Published var scheduled = 0 {
  didSet {
    Task {
      let systemCount = await systems.systems.count
      isCollaborating = scheduled > 0 && systemCount > 1
    }
  }
}
```

The starter project UI code will pick up `isCollaborating`'s value change, and then will play an animation onscreen while the property is set to `true`.

Build and run on all the iOS Simulators you're currently testing on. Then, tap **Engage systems** on one of the devices and enjoy the cool logo animation.

Your UI has really come alive! A connection indicator shows when devices connect, the animation shows when devices collaborate and, last but not least, the scheduled tasks indicator shows how the work spreads across devices. It's exhilarating to send a task to another machine and have it come back completed!

# Retrying failed tasks

While it might seem like your work in this chapter is done, there's one final task to take care of.

You've probably noticed that, thanks to the code you added in Chapter 7, "Concurrent Code With TaskGroup", you skip over any failed tasks and never return to them.

The code in **ScanTask.swift** calls `UnreliableAPI.action(failingEvery:)` to fail every tenth task so you can verify your error handling skills. Currently, when the local system fails, you catch the error and print a log message. When one of the remote systems fails to run the task, your request simply times out.

To wrap up SkyNet, you'll add new logic to retry failed tasks. After all, you don't want to miss any signs of alien life because one of the scans failed on the first try, do you?

Open **ScanModel.swift** and scroll to `runAllTasks()`. Here, you'll run your concurrent task group and expect each task to return a `Result<String, Error>`. `Result` helps you gracefully handle errors. You'll use the `Result.failure` case to print the error message to the output.

To retry failed tasks, you don't need the error; however, you need the task itself, so you can try running it again. To handle that, you'll add your own custom error type. Add the following anywhere inside `ScanModel`:

```
struct ScanTaskError: Error {
  let underlyingError: Error
  let task: ScanTask
}
```

This is especially useful for remotely executed tasks, which can fail for many reasons: shaky connections, timeouts and more.

Back in `runAllTasks()`, replace `Result<String, Error>.self` with `Result<String, ScanTaskError>.self`. This causes a few compile errors.

First, scroll to worker(number:system:) and change its return type from
Result<String, Error> to:

```
Result<String, ScanTaskError>
```

Then, in that same method, replace return .failure(error) with:

```
return .failure(.init(
  underlyingError: error,
  task: task
))
```

That takes care of the updates in worker(...). Now, scroll back to runAllTasks()
and find withThrowingTaskGroup(of: Result<String, Error>.self). Change
the error type like so:

```
withThrowingTaskGroup(of: Result<String, ScanTaskError>.self)
```

Then scroll just a bit down to your current error handling code:

```
case .failure(let error):
  print("Failed: \(error.localizedDescription)")
```

Here, you'll get the failed task and schedule it to execute on the local system once
again. Replace the current case with:

```
case .failure(let error):
  group.addTask(priority: .high) {
    print("Re-run task: \(error.task.input).",
          "Failed with: \(error.underlyingError)")
    return await self.worker(
      number: error.task.input,
      system: self.systems.localSystem)
  }
```

This addition will clear the final compile errors. As planned, if one task fails —
regardless if it's remote or local — you add a new task to the group and retry the scan
on the local system.

> **Note:** Speaking from experience, the best way to handle retrying tasks
> involves keeping track of how many times you've tried a task. It's annoying
> when a task always fails, but you keep retrying it indefinitely.
>
> Luckily, SkyNet will ultimately complete all the tasks that failed initially, so
> the current retrying logic will suffice.

Build and run. Look at the output console:

```
Completed: 11
Completed: 9 by Marin's iPod
Re-run task: 16. Failed with:
UnreliableAPI.action(failingEvery:) failed. <---
Completed: 12
Completed: 13 by Ted's iPhone
Completed: 14 by Ted's iPhone
Completed: 17
Completed: 15
Completed: 18
Completed: 16
Re-run task: 19. Failed with:
UnreliableAPI.action(failingEvery:) failed. <---
Completed: 19
Done.
```

You see that some of the remote tasks failed — timed out, really — and the app ran them locally once again to complete the full scan.

You also see that the app happily reports that it worked through the full batch of tasks:

With that last addition, your work here is truly done!

Congratulations on completing this final book project. There was a lot to take care of: an actor system, networking transport, replacing the model execution logic and plenty more!

# Key points

- An upcoming **distributed actor** language feature will allow developers to talk to remote actors almost as if they were local ones.

- There is a work-in-progress "Swift Distributed Actors" package for running actors on server clusters.

- Systems of distributed actors communicate over a **transport layer** that can use many different underlying services: local network, Bonjour, REST service, web socket and more.

- Thanks to **location transparency**, regardless of whether the actor method calls are relayed to another process or a different machine, you use a simple `await` call at the point of use.

- Building a custom distributed system isn't difficult once you implement the transport layer.

- In a system of distributed actors, each one needs a **unique address** so requests can be relayed reliably to the target peer and the responses delivered back to the original actor.

- Using distributed actors can fail for a myriad of reasons, so **asynchronous error handling** plays an even more significant role in such apps.

- Last but not least, a distributed app uses *the same APIs* as a local app: `async/await`, task groups and actors. The actor model allows for encapsulating the transport layer and keeping its implementation hidden from the API consumers.

# Where to go from here?

Completing this book is no small feat!

You started in Chapter 1, "Why Modern Swift Concurrency?", by writing some of your first async/await code and some pesky asynchronous tasks. Not long after that, you were already juggling tasks, continuations and asynchronous sequences — each furthering your understanding of the new concurrency model.

In the second half of the book, you moved forward with more advanced topics like testing, dynamic concurrency and — wait for it — actors. These ensure you're as concurrent as possible while avoiding some of the usual multithreading problems like data races and crashes.

By now, modern Swift concurrency should hold no secrets for you. If you have thoughts, questions or ideas you'd like to share with this book's readers, be sure to let us know in the book forums.

I'd like to leave you with this old proverb, which the Spider-Man comic books popularized. I think it's fitting for the last page of the book, given your newly acquired, vast knowledge of concurrent programming:

*"With great power comes great responsibility."*

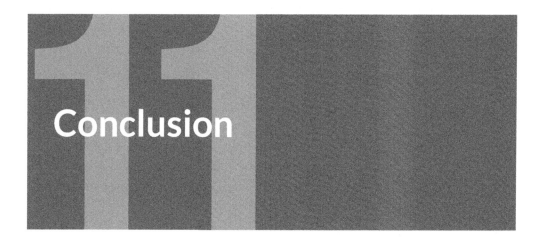

# Conclusion

You've made it! You should be super proud of yourself for completing this book. Concurrency can be a challenging topic to master, but that just makes your achievement that much sweeter. With your newly acquired knowledge, you are well poised to move on to trying some of Swift's new concurrency features in the real world.

As you start incorporating `async`/`await` into your app and leveraging the powerful modern concurrency features Swift offers, like **tasks** and **actors**, your app will become safer and more predictable when it reads and mutates your data concurrently. It will also become safer to reason about, because your code will "read synchronously" but run asynchronously.

We hope the concepts you've learned in this book helped you think differently about how to plan concurrent and parallel code in the modern world, while still keeping your sanity.

If you've enjoyed learning about the new modern concurrency features, you might also enjoy our book *Combine: Asynchronous Programming with Swift*. It showcases another modern variation for modeling and composing asynchronous work.

If you have any questions or comments as you work through this book, please stop by our forums at https://forums.raywenderlich.com and look for the particular forum category for this book.

Thank you again for purchasing this book. Your continued support is what makes the books, tutorials, videos and other things we do at raywenderlich.com possible. We truly appreciate it!

– The *Modern Concurrency in Swift* team

Made in the USA
Las Vegas, NV
05 November 2021